YOUR STORY MATTERS

YES IT DOES

YOUR STORY MATTERS

A SURPRISINGLY PRACTICAL
GUIDE TO WRITING

BY

RICHARD
SCRIMGER

WITH ILLUSTRATIONS BY
D. McFADZEAN

tundra

Tundra Books, an imprint of Tundra Book Group,
a division of Penguin Random House of Canada Limited

Library and Archives Canada Cataloguing in Publication

Title: Your story matters : a surprisingly practical guide to writing /
written by Richard Scrimger; illustrated by D. McFadzean.
Names: Scrimger, Richard, 1957- author. | McFadzean, D., illustrator.
Identifiers: Canadiana (print) 20230542476 | Canadiana (ebook) 20230542492 |
ISBN 9781770498426 (hardcover) | ISBN 9781770498471 (EPUB)
Subjects: LCSH: Authorship—Juvenile literature. |
LCSH: Creative writing—Juvenile literature.
Classification: LCC PN159 .S37 2024 | DDC j808.02—dc23

Published simultaneously in the United States of America by Tundra Books
of Northern New York, an imprint of Tundra Book Group, a division of
Penguin Random House of Canada Limited

Library of Congress Control Number: 2023946907

Edited by Samantha Swenson and Katelyn Chan
Designed by John Martz
Typeset by Sean Tai
The text was set in Caslon.

Printed in Canada

www.penguinrandomhouse.ca

1 2 3 4 5   28 27 26 25 24

Penguin
Random House
tundra | TUNDRA BOOKS

For everyone who's ever sat in a gym or library
or classroom and listened to me talk about writing.
Thank you.

There are three rules for writing a novel.
Unfortunately, no one knows what they are.

W. SOMERSET MAUGHAM

Mostly a true book, with some stretchers,
as I said before.

MARK TWAIN, *THE ADVENTURES OF HUCKLEBERRY FINN*

CONTENTS

INTRODUCTION: HI THERE!

How you doing? I see you're holding my book. Maybe you're looking forward to reading it. Maybe you're only reading because you have to. Either way, let's get acquainted. I'm Richard. You're you. Glad to meet you.

Yes I am.

This book is about story. As you read, you will learn what I mean by story, and why stories are important. You'll learn what makes a good story, and where good stories come from. We'll talk about one or two of my stories, and then we'll get to the actual writing. You'll learn how to start a story. What — and what not — to put in it. How to end it. And how to make it better when you rewrite it. We will build your story together. (You'll do the actual work. I'll be cheering you on.)

Once you know more about story, you'll have a better understanding of what's going on when you open a book, or turn on the TV, or pick up a game controller. And the next story you write will be better than your last one.

Along the way, we'll have some fun. That's the thing about stories — they're more *fun* than a lot of other stuff you learn in school. Science can be cool. (Things blow up!) French or Arabic or Mandarin can be useful. (*Où est la salle de bain?*) Math is satisfying when you get it right, like doing a jigsaw puzzle. But none of these subjects are really *fun.* When you were a kid, did you snuggle up to listen to bedtime verbs? Did you look forward to bedtime experiments? Did you beg for just one more bedtime fraction?

Didn't think so.

Ready to have some fun? Me too.

PART 1
PREPARING

CHAPTER 1
STORIES MATTER

Story goes back a long, long, long way.

Maybe the very first words were practical. Words for *fire*, or *rock*, or *friend*. Words that meant *Watch out!* Or *It's my turn!* Or *Thanks for dinner!* But as soon as we stopped using every waking minute to stay alive — as soon as we had any spare time — we told stories. We sat around the fire and swapped ideas. Ideas like *I think that's how the world was made.* Or *I wonder where that big yellow light in the sky went.* Or *Who's afraid of the advancing wall of ice?*

We're still telling stories today. More than ever. Books, TV shows, movies, video games — stories are everywhere. You'll spend your life with them. Maybe you won't write stories for a living, but you'll spend lots of time reading them, watching them, acting them out.

That's why understanding story is important. The more you know about something, the more fun you can have with it. Imagine turning on the TV to watch giants in plastic armor run up and down a striped field fighting over the possession of a small prolate spheroid. You can't really enjoy a sport until you know what the players are trying to do. What's the point of it all?

Stories don't have "rules" like football, but there's always a point to them. The more you understand what the writer is trying to do, the more you'll get out of the story. This book will make you a better writer. It will also make you a better reader, a better TV watcher, a better gamer.

Good news: All stories are built the same way. A *SpongeBob SquarePants* episode, a Star Wars movie, a Shakespeare play and a story you wrote in second grade are all made from the same basic ingredients. As we go through this book, I'll show you how to use these ingredients to make a story. And every time you watch TV or play a video game, you'll notice them. You'll understand how the story hangs together.

There's another reason why stories matter. This one is kind of serious. Hang on a minute while I put on my important pants and comb my hair. OK.

Stories give you a peek into someone else's life — someone who may not look or talk or act like you. Someone with different problems than yours. By reading their story, you can learn a bit about what it's like to be them. And that is important. We are a diverse community. We succeed when we get along with each other. And the best way to get along with someone is to learn about them. To walk in their shoes for a few pages. Stories show you what it's like to be a princess or a peasant. To have a superpower or a wheelchair or a dying parent. To find yourself trapped in a dungeon or in another world or in a family who doesn't understand you. Sharing stories makes us a better community.

Whew. That got a bit deep, didn't it? Sorry if your eyes glazed over.

Let's get started. Where do these ideas come from? Where does a story begin?

Glad you asked. But before we dive right in . . .

QUIZ

That's right. Most textbooks wait until you've done a few exercises and memorized a few rules before giving you a test. Not me. I don't like rules.

TRUE OR FALSE?

1. A Superman comic is a story.

2. *Minecraft* is a story.

3. A banana is a story.

4. Your story matters.

5. The most important rule about being a good person is DON'T BE MEAN. (I know we didn't talk about being good. So what? You should know this anyway.)

Answers to the quiz are on the next page.

ANSWERS TO QUIZ

They're all TRUE except Question 3. You can make a story *about* a banana, but no piece of fruit is a story in itself.

The point I want to draw your attention to involves Question 4. Everyone's story matters. Which means that *your* story matters. Yes it does.

The story you write while working through this book probably won't sell millions of copies and get made into a movie (though it might!), but your ideas about life and love, space and time, homework and pimples, zombies and older sisters and laundry — all the ideas you share — make the community a better place.

You matter. Your story matters.

OK, let's get to work.

NO PIECE OF FRUIT IS A STORY IN ITSELF.

CHAPTER 2
ONE RULE

Let's start with a basic definition. What is a story? What makes a *story* different from, say, that *banana*? Or a *feeling*? Or an *aunt*? What must a story have in it? Go on. What do you think?

A beginning, a middle and an end?

Stories have beginnings and middles and ends, but so does a piece of string, and a piece of string is not a story. Try again. What must a story have?

Words?

No again. Lots of stories are told without using any words. *Fantasia* is one of my favorite movies and there's not a word in it. On the other hand, there are words on a cereal box, and a cereal box is not much of a story.

I'm not going to draw this out. Most of you know it anyway. The key ingredients of a story are setting, plot and characters. A story has to take place somewhere, with something happening to someone.

Here's a story. It's short, but it ticks all the boxes:

Aunt Mary Lee (someone) *drives down Main Street to the supermarket* (somewhere). *She buys a loaf of bread and a jar of peanut butter, drives home and makes a sandwich* (something happening).

That's a story. Is it a good story? No.

So what makes a good story? Why do we like some stories more than others?

Here's where we get to the rule. There is only one rule to telling a good story: DON"T BE BORING.

There are no other rules.

Seriously. If you Google "story writing rules" you'll get — let's see — 478,000,000 results (in 0.58 seconds!). They aren't rules. They're ideas. Suggestions. Hey, I'll be making some suggestions in this book. I've been writing longer than you have, and I know enough to teach you about it. At least, that's what I told my publisher. (And they believed me. Suckers!)

But if you ignore every one of my suggestions and every one of the 478,000,000 online articles, and still write something I want to read more of? That's a good story.

Don't be boring. Who wants to read a boring story? Nobody. Not me. Not you. Not even your mom. That story you wrote back in second grade, the one with the dog and the hat — she only stuck it on the fridge door because she loves you.

Let's examine why "Aunt Mary Lee Goes to the Store" is a bad story. What is the story starter? Why does she go to the store? Because she's hungry. Is that boring? Not at all. Hunger can be a fine story starter. The hero of *Les Misérables* is so hungry he steals a loaf of bread. The difference between Jean Valjean and Aunt Mary Lee is that he gets in trouble and she doesn't.

This. Is. Important.

For a story not to be boring — for a story to work — something has to go wrong.

That might be the single biggest lesson in cooking up a story. I'll say it again and again throughout this book. I'll say it in different ways.

There is no story without a problem.

We can improve Mary Lee's story by giving her a problem. How about this one: *What if she runs out of gas and has to call a tow truck?*

Still kind of boring. A story problem shouldn't be solved fast. Jean Valjean goes to jail for stealing a loaf of bread, escapes, and then is on the run for about eight hundred pages. Let's give Mary Lee a bigger problem:

What if there's a mouse inside the bread bag, and Aunt Mary Lee screams and faints from shock?

That's a little better, isn't it? There are possibilities. She could complain to the board of health and get the store closed down. The mouse could bite her and give her a rare disease. She could end up in hospital and fall in love with her nurse. And we're not out of ideas yet. Vermin are a real-world problem. I have a soft spot for unexpected, magical problems. *What if Aunt Mary Lee buys bread with an ingredient that turns her invisible?*

Now we're talking. Aunt Mary Lee could end up joining the Marvel Universe!

Pay attention to the phrase that starts off those suggestions: *What if . . .*

I use that phrase a lot in this book. *What if* is the best question to ask when you're thinking of writing a story. Stories come from your imagination. *What if* is what imagination is made of. You know how you're 90 percent water? (Or is it 60 percent? Whatever — there's a lot of water in you.) Imagination is 90 percent *what if.*

Because we have different imaginations, we will come up with different *what ifs.* Your story won't be the same as mine. Which is why we should read each other's stories. Which is why your story matters. Yes it does.

———

But, I hear you say.

But wait.

But how . . . I mean —

But where exactly *do stories come from?*

Your imagination.

Where do you look for that?

An imagination is not like a spleen or a big toe. You can't point to it.

Is there a brain treasure map, where X *marks the spot where all the stories are? Can you* imagine *your imagination? What does it look like? How do you navigate it?*

Read the next chapter and find out.

CHAPTER 3

FEELINGS

According to the dictionary, *imagination* means "forming mental images of what is not actually there."

Mental images. Like, pictures. You could think of your imagination as a collage, with scraps of memory and feelings and fantasy pasted together on a giant piece of cardboard. Or you could see it as a stew with lots of tastes: spicy, sweet, salty, umami (a word I just learned). Or as a junk drawer, with everything from scissors to dental floss to gummy bears to car keys to sunglasses to . . . well . . . whatever.

I think of imagination as a closet full of stuff to play with. A lot of it is fun. Imagination is fantasy, right? *What if this cool, amazing, magical thing happened?* Your imagination might have some superheroes in it. What else is in there? Ice cream that makes you taller, BFFs, pants that fit perfectly, goals and home runs and league championships, plane trips to faraway places, and TV shows starring you. Ahhh. All those amazing *what ifs*.

I THINK OF IMAGINATION AS A CLOSET FULL OF STUFF TO PLAY WITH.

But imagination is also fear. *What if this terrible, awful, horrible, scary, diabolical thing happened?* Remember those creepy dolls your grandma gave you that kept you awake for two nights? They're in the imagination closet too. My friend Miriam had a stuffed bear with one weird dead eye. (We hid it at the back of the closet and then shut the door.) On my tenth birthday, my uncle Jim gave me a bar of soap shaped like a human tongue. (Really. Still makes me shudder.) What kind of terrible things are lurking in your imagination? Bruising bullies and fake friends who lie about you? Slime that oozes, poison that drips, zombies that lurch? Swarms of bees, spaghetti-nests of snakes, or the dead of night that lasts forever while your parents scream? Roomfuls of people laughing at you because you've done something embarrassing and shameful and stupid?

Wow, that got grim, didn't it? Let's go back to crafting your story.

Your imagination is full of *what ifs*. But beware. If you pick *what ifs* at random and start writing, you might get overwhelmed by all the choices. Here's what can happen:

What if I was walking down the street and ran into a mugger — no, wait, what if I found an abandoned baby in a stroller — no, not a baby, a dragon — no, no, what if I met myself from the future . . . and I decided to run — no, to call the cops — no, to go back to the future . . . but the dragon set fire to my pants, and the portal was closing . . . no, wait, the baby in the carriage was me from the past, and the dragon was my babysitter, and my pants were . . .

It's like you opened an overstuffed closet, and everything fell out. How do you choose? What kind of idea is best to build a story on?

I wish I could give you an answer, a surefire story starter: *Close your eyes, spin around, say your favorite author's name backward and you'll get a bestselling idea.*

I've tried that. It doesn't work. Sorry.

Sometimes you get lucky. Sometimes a really good story idea will flash across your mind out of nowhere, like a rainbow across a corner of the sky. *What if a magical camera turned you into the person you took a picture of?* Not bad, eh? Or how about this: *What if the new kid sitting beside you in class turned out to be a zombie?* Those ideas both came to me in a flash — two flashes — and the flashes started me off on two books.

I can't tell you where in the sky to look for a rainbow. They can show up anywhere. So keep your eyes open. Notice things. Observe the world around you. Listen to a podcast, or a new piece of music, or your grandmother's stories about when she was a little girl. Pay attention to the news. Read something.

Ideas are like a good kind of infection. The more you expose yourself to them, the better your chance of catching one.

Waiting for a good idea can take time. But maybe you have to write a story for next week. Or tomorrow. Maybe you're hoping my book will help.

Good news. The point of this book is to show you how to write a story *now*. Here's a hack — a way to skip some steps and find your story. Ready?

What if is something you make up. It's a kind of lie. And the most powerful lies are the ones that start with truth. My hack is to look inside yourself for something you truly care about. It's harder to be boring when you care.

There are three feelings that offer ways into story. Three basic feelings. Three primal feelings.

Note: they're all dark. If you're trying to come up with a story, don't look inside yourself for how happy you were when you got a puppy, or how much you love your favorite dessert — unless you end up choking on your apple crisp or Rover chews up your new shoes. Remember, there's no story unless something goes wrong.

Here are the feelings that lead to story. Let's talk about them one at a time.

FEAR

There's a reason horror movies and scary stories are popular. We've all been scared. To kick-start your story planning, look inside yourself for what scares you. If you believe ghosts are scary, you can tell a great ghost story.

Maybe it's not ghosts. Are you afraid of the dark? Of being trapped underground? Maybe you're afraid of what

happens when you die. Eternal nothingness and eternal torment both sound pretty yucky, don't they?

When you write about what scares you, you'll care about what's happening even if the events in your story aren't real. You've never been buried alive, but if the idea makes your palms sweat, you'll tell a convincing story because you'll be as scared as your hero.

Take spiders. Lots of people are scared of them. My daughter, for instance. She could write a scary story about them, because she's panic-stricken when she sees one.

Know who else could write a scary spider story? J.R.R. Tolkien. There was a childhood spider incident he never got over. But that fear served him well. Think about Bilbo being attacked by spiders in Mirkwood Forest in *The Hobbit*, or that scene at the end of *The Two Towers* where Frodo and Sam are crawling into Mordor and meet the mother of all spiders, Shelob.

I couldn't write that scene. I like spiders. I had a pet daddy longlegs when I was a kid. (I know now that they aren't really spiders, but I didn't then.) Not much of a pet. It didn't do tricks or come when I called it. I would take it down from the window ledge on rainy afternoons and watch it run across my desk. Yes, I know, I was a weird kid. If I had written that scene, Sam would nudge Frodo and say, "Look, Master Frodo, a giant spider." Frodo would smile and say, "Aww, isn't she cute?" Then he'd walk forward, talking to Shelob the way you talk to a puppy. "Who's a cute spider? Whooooo's a cute spider? Yes, you are. Yes, you are!" And Shelob would pounce and eat them both up.

Tolkien did it better.

I am not fearless — no one is. When I was in seventh grade, my best friend's parents went through a messy divorce. I hated hearing them yelling at each other — it sounded so mean! And what if my parents started acting like that? Also, there was a gang of eighth graders who went around the schoolyard teasing people about their clothes: baggy shorts, old shoes, the same shirt three days in a row — stuff like that. They called the game "Spot the Loser," and I was afraid they would pick on me because I was guilty of all those fashion no-nos. Also, there was a girl who both attracted and paralyzed me. She was bigger and more athletic than I was, and she had a habit of nibbling the end of her pencil that I found incredibly fetching.

Did I face my fears? Did I call out my friend's parents? *Mr. and Mrs. Spielman, you are behaving very, very badly — stop it at once!* Did I march over to the fashion police and defend the lonely kid they were picking on? *Leave him alone! You're the real losers! You want to laugh at someone, how about me? I haven't changed these jeans all week!* Did I saunter over to the athletic and charming Robin, pretend shoot her with my fingers, and say something suave?

No. I didn't do anything. I wasn't scared of ghosts or spiders, but I was afraid of other people's anger and meanness. I was afraid of being yelled at or teased.

Decades later, I looked inside myself, found my old fears and gave them to the thirteen-year-old hero of one of my first books, *The Nose from Jupiter*. Alan's life includes parents even angrier than my friend's, playground nasties even meaner than mine, and a girl he really likes. And he's not doing anything about these problems because — just like me — he's afraid.

I started with this truth and asked, *What if things were different? What if I wasn't — or a part of me wasn't — afraid?* And I came up with the character of Norbert, a tiny alien who comes to live in Alan's nose. (I know that sounds wacky. But the inside of your nose is a big place. You didn't know that?) The key to the story is that Norbert is NOT AFRAID. Not of Alan's parents, or the bullies, or the girl. He says what he thinks, just like I wished I could have done back when I was thirteen.

That's what you can do in a story: You can change the past. You can revisit the bad things that happened and make them different.

Let's go on to our next story-building feeling. Like fear, it's dark. And universal. And —

Wait. One last thing about fear. Fear can be funny. We've all been scared, and we've all been *embarrassed*.

Embarrassment is fear lite. You're not afraid of getting hurt or getting in big trouble. You're just afraid of looking like an idiot. That's why I didn't walk over to Robin and say, "Hey there, dollface, do you have a Band-Aid for the knee I scraped when I fell for you?" I didn't think she'd beat me up (though she sure could have), but she might have burst out laughing.

Look inside. Your scaredest moment is a good story hack. So is your most embarrassing moment.

Can you think of another dark and universal feeling? Sure you can. Let's talk about it.

SADNESS

Maybe it's great to be you. Every day you eat your favorite meals and ace the test and win the race and go home to watch your favorite shows. You share your good news with your family and pets and friends, who are all so happy for you that, after the best dinner ever, you all squeeze together in a group hug that lasts the whole evening long, and you go to bed with a smile glued on your face because it's been just a perfect day, and you wake up the next morning still smiling because it's going to be another one.

If that's your life (which I doubt), good for you. But it makes a dull story, don't you think? Who wants to read about someone who spends all their time smiling and winning? We might want to live in this kind of paradise, but we don't want to hear about it.

We've all felt sad. Sadness is about *loss*, and we've all lost stuff. One of literature's three basic storylines (more on this later) is SOMEBODY LOSES SOMETHING.

Think of the things you used to have that you don't have anymore. Little things — the bike that got stolen, the book or game your friend says you never gave them even though you know better, the phone you were sure was in *this* pocket and now isn't. Think of bigger things — your pet dying, your grandma getting sick, your best friend moving away, your parents splitting up. And there are even bigger things than that, as some of you know well. The world's full of loss, and no one gets out of here alive. Loss is a great place to start a story. Find yours, and ask yourself, *What if it was different?*

I did that in my book *Downside Up*. Some of the saddest moments in my life came around the time my dog Casey died. I went back to that time and asked myself, *What if my dog was alive somewhere, and there was a way to see him again?* I came up with a portal to a parallel world, with dragons and a twin me and all sorts of other shenanigans. They were all made up. But the feelings were real.

Remember how I said that your scaredest moment was a good place to find a story? So is your saddest moment. What have you lost? Check into that.

If you're going to write about loss, here's one key point to remember about a story involving loss: YOU CAN'T LOSE WHAT YOU DON'T HAVE. If you're going to write a sad story about losing your cat, Funky (years ago when my kids were little, we had a cat with that name), it's a good idea to introduce Funky to the reader so we get a sense of what a cute, cuddly, frisky pal she is. Then when Funky gets run over by a moving van or eaten by a coyote, we'll feel bad. If you open the story with Funky getting squished, it's harder for us to care about her. We're more likely to gasp and maybe giggle, aren't we? The cat is so darn flat. Just like little Susie. Oh, wait — I haven't told you that story yet. You'll see what I mean later.

OK, we've done FEAR and SADNESS. There's one more story feeling. Can you guess what it is? You can't? Really? What's wrong with you? You got rocks in your head? (One of my dad's favorite questions to me, growing up. It always made me feel . . .)

ANGER

Ever been angry? Of course you have. Your little sister borrows your favorite pair of jeans without asking, so you scream at her. Your parents won't let you go to Spencer's sleepover party, so you stomp off to your room and slam the door. The price of licorice twists goes up, so you grump at the store clerk. The group at your lunch table laughs because your food looks different than theirs.

Grrrrrr.

Some of this anger is misdirected. It's not the store clerk's fault that the price went up. Your parents are right to be worried about Spencer's parties — you lost your shoes at the last one, remember? You never did get them back. As for your sister, she may be a brat, but you have some of her stuff, too, don't you? What about that striped top that looks way better on you? You know the one.

But laughing at someone's food for being different is not much different than laughing at *them* for being different, and that stinks. It wouldn't matter if they (whoever they are) were laughing at you or at someone else, it still stinks. You'd be right to feel angry.

The way I see it, there are two basic types of villains —
bullies and sneaks. Think of two wolves: the one in "The
Three Little Pigs" and the one in "Little Red Riding
Hood." Those are the two types of villains.

The bully threatens in the open. You see what's
going on. *Do this — or else! Open the door or I'll blow your
house down. Give me your lunch money or I'll hit you. Go
along with the group or else we'll turn against you.* Cyber-
bullying isn't a punch in the nose, but it's just as violent
and scary.

The sneak insinuates, whispers, lies, steals. You don't
see what's happening until it's too late, and you wonder
where your favorite socks went or what happened to your
reputation.

So what do you do about villains? How can you deal
with them?

In real life, villains often get away with it. Teachers
aren't always around to mete out playground justice. A
bad picture of you can go viral and make you wish the
earth would swallow you up.

Villains often succeed when they grow up too. Their
need — for money, power, attention — drives them hard.
They'll go further and be less generous than regular folks.
All the tyrants in history were bullies.

But they do not have to win in a story. Little Red and
the three pigs do better than the wolves. Is there a villain

in your life? Use your anger. Channel it. Work through it to *revenge*.

Sounds wrong, eh? Revenge? Your folks aren't going to like that. But there's lots of great revenge writing. I don't know how J.D. Salinger felt, or how Deborah Ellis or Sapphire feel, but Holden Caulfield's character is angry, and so are Parvana's and Claireece Jones's.

Revenge may or may not be sweet; it may or may not be the Lord's; it may or may not be a dish best served cold; but it is for sure a great story builder.

I use it myself. Despite being a chubby know-it-all with glasses, I was never bullied. (I told jokes and shared my candy.) But I was scared of the big bad wolves and aware of their power. I worried about what would happen to me if I stopped being funny. My characters Mary in *The Nose from Jupiter*, the dad in *Me & Death* and the dog in *Zomboy* are all based on bullies I have known.

Here's a slightly different take: I was at a middle school not that long ago, giving a presentation to a big group. I talked about anger and how to use it. "Is there someone in your life who drives you crazy?" I asked them. "Someone who lies and cheats, who has a tantrum every time they don't get their way and somehow turns themselves into the victim? Someone who makes you so mad you want to explode? Next story you write, use your

anger. Put that special someone into your story, and have something bad happen to them."

I've used this line before. It usually gets a laugh. Not this time. The strangest thing happened. There was a collective sigh, and everyone in the gym turned around and looked in the same direction. Obviously, there was a kid back there that everyone thought of as an awful person.

Immediately, I felt *sorry* for the kid. I didn't know anything about them. But the idea of being resented by everyone in the school spoke to me. Talk about being outnumbered in your life!

I don't think I'm a meanie (my kids might disagree), but I know what it's like to be alone. I could put myself into that mean kid's shoes. As a matter of fact, I am writing a story about one right now. (Well, not RIGHT now — right now I'm writing this. But I've finished my first draft and my editor likes it. It might even be published before this book.)

That's all I have to say about emotional starting places for now. Before we move on, let's review. No quiz this time. More of a chat.

Feelings are a good way into a story. But not just any feelings. Since you want your story to have something go wrong, the best story builders are the feelings that come from or lead to something going wrong: *dark* feelings. Go into your memory closet and find a moment when you felt sad, or mad, or scared, or embarrassed. The thing doesn't have to have happened to you, but you have to care about it. Your baby brother fell in the swimming pool, and you were scared for him. Your best friend farted loudly in the middle of their presentation, and you were embarrassed for them. (Though, let's be honest, you were probably howling with laughter.)

To turn your feeling into a story, ask yourself the question: *What if things were different?* I'll have more to say about that later.

CHAPTER 4

PLAN. A. HEAD.

This book is about story. So far it's been all theory — what story is, why it matters, how to find a story you care about.

Theory is important, but so is practice. Once you have a story you *want* to write, you have to figure out how to go about it.

There are no rules about what makes a good story except that it should be interesting. So, there are no rules to *writing* a good story except that the result should be something people want to read.

No rules. But I have a suggestion.

Plan ahead.

That's what my youngest used to say, back when he was in kindergarten and I was starting to clean the house or make dinner. "I have three words for you, Dad," he'd say. "Plan. A. Head."

Think of your story like a vacation. You've thought about *where* you'll go — Disneyland, say, or Paris, or the beach. But you're probably not going to have a great time if you just hop in the car and drive off. You want to plan how to get there, where to stay, what to wear. Stuff like that.

It's the same with a story. Make a plan. Novels and TV series involve extensive plans. So do shorter pieces. Even a seven-minute cartoon like "Bully for Bugs" (a personal favorite) went through an exhaustive process of scripting, storyboarding and editing. Your story — the one we're talking about in this book — should start with a plan. You want to be clear about where you're going and how you'll get there. After all, knowing what *kind* of vacation you're going on helps you pack, right? You'd bring different stuff to Paris than you would to the beach.

A few pages ago, I mentioned the three basic storylines in literature and promised that there'd be more later. Well, now it's later. Every story follows one or more of those storylines. Yours will too. You can think of them as guides or templates when you make your plan.

Here are the three basic stories:

1. The stranger plot:
   Our hero meets a stranger and stuff happens.

2. The journey plot:
   Our hero goes on a journey and stuff happens.

3. The loss plot:
   Our hero loses something and stuff happens.

YOU WANT TO PLAN HOW TO GET THERE, WHERE TO STAY, WHAT TO WEAR.

You don't start by *choosing* one of these plots. But knowing the kind of story you're writing will help you plan ahead.

Run through stories you know, and slot them into the three basic story plans. In *The Cat in the Hat*, our two heroes meet an unusual stranger, and lots of stuff happens. Sky Woman falls through space onto the back of Great Turtle and the world happens. Little Red Riding Hood meets a sly stranger. Snow White meets seven little strangers. Dorothy goes to Oz. Lucy goes to Narnia. The Little Mermaid loses her voice. The Beast loses his good looks. Romeo and Juliet lose their hearts.

Of course, most stories involve more than one of the three plotlines. Adam and Eve meet a snaky stranger and lose paradise. Cinderella meets her fairy godmother and loses her slipper. Rapunzel loses her freedom and meets a prince. Dorothy's journey — and Odysseus's and Jonah's and Lara Croft's and the Rythulian Traveler's — are full of strangers and lost things.

ASSIGNMENT #1: STORY PLANNING

This is a practical book. I talk about story in general, but I want you to be able to use what I say to write an actual story. The assignments in this book will walk you through the story-writing process step-by-step. Here's the first step: make an outline. We'll do one together.

This practice outline will be a version of the stranger plot. Our hero (a kid) meets a stranger (a dog) and stuff happens.

What kind of stuff? Well, that's the whole point. The *stuff* makes up the story. I've workshopped "Hero Meets Dog" all over the country, and in a few other countries as well. Hundreds of audiences have come up with hundreds of different *stuff* — hundreds of versions of the story.

Every single version works. A few are amazing. I remember one workshop in vivid detail, even down to the way the student with the goofy idea — his name was Ralph — looked and talked. I like Ralph's answer so much that I often end my presentations or speeches with a reference to it.

So here it goes. We'll do it like the page of a comic book — a storyboard. Take a piece of paper and divide it into six sections. Then, in each of the six sections, draw or write what happens. Like this:

You may ask yourself, *How does this assignment help me with my story? I'm not writing about a dog.*

We'll get to your story, I promise. This is practice. Like music practice. Running C-sharp minor triads up and down the piano isn't playing *Moonlight Sonata*, it's practice for when you do play it. The Karate Kid washes the car as practice for his fight moves. *Wax on, wax off.* (Do you know that? Classic movie, popular show. And a great metaphor for practice.)

Here's how I would fill the grid:

"HERO MEETS DOG"

HERO WALKING	DOG STANDING
DOG BLOCKING HERO	DOG ATTACKS, KNOCKING HERO TO GROUND
EARTHQUAKE! DUST CLOUD. FALLEN TREES. GROUND IN FRONT OF HERO HAS DROPPED AWAY.	HERO AND DOG STAND ON EDGE OF DISASTER. REALIZING DOG HAS SAVED THE DAY, HERO PETS DOG.

This isn't the only possible plot, of course. Different story-lines would work as well. Maybe the dog chases our hero out of the park. Maybe the dog steals our hero's Frisbee and runs off, with the hero chasing him. Maybe a bolt of lightning hits hero and dog at the same time and they swap bodies.

Notice how all possible plots involve something going wrong. Another way to think about this is *conflict*. Conflict doesn't have to go so far as war, or even a fight (though wars and fights are conflicts). In story, something going wrong is conflict. An earthquake is a conflict. A plane crash is a conflict. Your family arguing about what to watch on TV is a conflict. In a conflict, different sides (in this case, the hero and the dog) want different things.

Your turn now. Fill in the grid the way you want to. Get used to moving your characters around so that stuff happens. Make sure there's some conflict. Without conflict there's no story.

I'll meet you on the next page when you're finished.

———

Was that fun? I hope so. It was also useful practice. Put aside the outline for now. We'll come back to it in a bit.

So far, we've talked about stories in general. It's time to start thinking about *your* story. What are *you* going to say?

PART 2
MODELING

CHAPTER 5
IMITATION

Thinking and planning are important steps in the writing process. But sooner or later you have to write those first sentences. Story ideas are made from your experience and imagination. But the story itself is made of words and phrases, which are technical in the literal meaning of the word — they are a matter of technique.

Let's talk about the technique of writing. We learn by imitation. Babies watch their parents' mouths, trying to make the same sounds. We learn to tie our shoes, write the alphabet, throw a ball, stir a pot — all sorts of basic life skills — by imitating.

Writers learn by mimicking their favorite authors' styles, in the same way that bands or DJs try to recreate the sounds they enjoy listening to. When asked for advice by aspiring writers, I answer: "Read." Then I add: "When you find a story you like, try to write one yourself that *looks* like it."

I don't mean copying, with your hero's name substituted for Pippi Longstocking's or Pecola Breedlove's or Frenchie's. *Examine* the stories. How do we find out how strong Pippi is? How long is the physical description of Pecola? When do we learn why they call him Frenchie? How soon does the trouble start? And so on. Use what you learn from your favorite author in your story.

Let's talk some more about imitation as a technique. I'll write a story, then break it into pieces to show you what I mean. It'll be fun and easy. (Well, it'll be easy anyway.)

The Story

You're always the star of your own life, but you're not always a hero. Some days you're a clown. Take that Saturday morning when I was ten years old, living downtown, watching cartoons . . .

When I say imitating, I don't mean your story should start with you watching cartoons. Imitation is not stealing. Your story is about you, not me. Our stories are different. Ahem.

. . . living downtown, watching cartoons with my little brother. . . .

By the way, this part is true. I have a younger brother, and we did live downtown. These days you can watch cartoons anytime you want, but when I was a kid, they only ran on Saturday and Sunday mornings. I'll come back to the true and not-true parts of my story later. Moving on.

. . . cartoons with my little brother. I got a phone call from my mom. She sounded excited.
"Richard!" she said. . . .

You know what? I've wrecked the start. I didn't even give the story a title. I'm going to get another cup of coffee. When I come back, I'll start again.

———

The Story: "Subway Surprise" (take #2)

You're always the star of your own life, but you're not always a hero. Some days you're a clown. Take that Saturday morning when I was ten years old, living downtown, watching cartoons in the living room with my little brother. I got a phone call from my mom. She sounded excited.

"Richard!" she said. "You and David have to come quick. There's a sale!"

My mom loved to save money. It was a hobby of hers. She liked saving money the way I liked watching cartoons and eating rice pudding.

"Aw, Ma!" I said.

"Willie's Clothing Outlet has winter coats half off! Come now and try them on. Otherwise I'll just buy the biggest sizes, and you'll have to wear them."

"No, no!" I protested. "I don't want a coat that's too big! My friends will laugh —"

"Get on the subway. If you're here in twenty minutes, I'll take you to lunch at Fran's Restaurant."

Mood changer! I loved Fran's. "With rice pudding for dessert?"

"Get off at St Andrew Station and walk three blocks. Willie's is right there! Twenty minutes! Starting from now!"

I wanted a coat that fit and lunch at Fran's. So did my little brother. We ran down the street to the subway station and hopped on the next southbound train.

Our car was mostly empty. Stations went by. Dave and I amused ourselves by "surfing" — standing with our legs spread like we were on surfboards.

The idea was to not lose your balance as the subway squealed and swayed around the corners.

Even though he was two years younger, Dave was a better surfer than me. "Ha ha!" he said whenever I stumbled. Dave liked to point out what you were doing wrong.

We came to King Station, the second to last one before St Andrew. We were in good time. I could practically taste the rice pudding. The subway doors opened. And then —

Onto our car walked the biggest, scariest, meanest-looking guy I had ever seen. I know stereotypes are misleading. Some of the scariest-looking people are really nice. Some of the cutest people are really mean. But this guy — WOW! Creepy as a pocket full of leeches. He was a big dude, with narrow eyes and thick, dark eyebrows that came down in an angry *V*. He had ears that stuck way out of his bald head and drooped under the weight of the earrings that stitched them. It was fall and kind of cool outside, but he only wore a shirt, which was tight enough that you could see he had biceps like cantaloupes. He inhaled noisily, glaring around. Anger radiated off this guy like heat. Maybe that's why he was so lightly dressed.

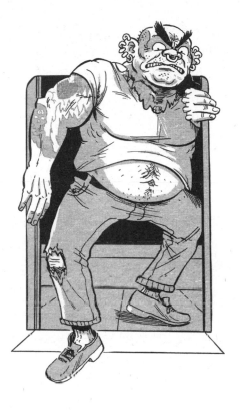

Tension inside the subway car went way up, like a barbecue when you squeeze fuel onto it. The guy threw himself down next to an old lady, who immediately moved to another seat.

Sorry to interrupt. This is part one, the SETUP of the story. We'll talk about structural stuff later. For now, put a pin here as we move on to part two, the middle, which I call MAKING THINGS WORSE.

The subway jerked as it started up again. I didn't want to attract the creepy guy's attention, so I found a seat and tried to make myself smaller.

"Ha ha! You lose!" said Dave. He had his arms out to keep balance.

"Sit down!" I whispered. I didn't want my brave but foolish little brother drawing attention to us.

The atmosphere in the car was tense all the way to the next station. The doors opened. Everyone but us got off. Dave noticed the creepy guy and, being Dave, had to say something.

"Hey! You've got a picture on your neck." He pointed. "See that, Rich? This guy looks weird, eh?"

Neck tattoos, like multiple earrings, weren't very common back then.

"Shhhh," I whispered. Too late.

"You talking about me?" The guy's voice sounded like boulders grinding together.

Should I grab Dave and pull him off the train? We might be late for Mom, but being on time seemed less important now.

I thought about that — for too long. The doors closed, and the train started again. Our station was the next one.

The creepy guy lurched over to my brother,

who was still standing in the middle of the car with his arms out. Dave came up to the guy's belly button, and weighed about as much as one of his legs.

I tried to hurry the train up in my mind. "Come on!" I muttered. "Come on, come on!"

"Why are you talking about me?" the guy growled.

"Because you're funny-looking," said Dave. He wasn't scared at all. I was. I gasped.

The big ugly angry scary guy seemed to swell up like a balloon. He reached down and grabbed Dave's arm.

"Hey!" Dave struggled to get free. The creepy guy's V-shaped eyebrows lifted. His mouth twisted. Was he smiling? It was hard to tell.

"Ouch!" said Dave.

The creep's big belly moved up and down. He was laughing. And Dave was in pain.

Oh no. Oh no oh no oh no! I couldn't let my brother be torn limb from limb. Somebody had to do something. But who? And what?

"Stop!" a strained, high-pitched voice shouted. Whose voice? Mine. I didn't recognize myself. "Leave him alone, you bully!" I shouted.

He looked up at me.

Up?

Yes. He had to look up because I was standing on the seat.

This was an emergency. So I decided to use the subway emergency system. You know the yellow emergency strip that runs around every car? Press it and an alarm goes off at headquarters. The doors lock and the cops come to investigate at the next stop.

That was my plan.

"Let him go," I said, "or I'll press this emergency strip!"

Another quick interruption. This is the end of part two, the MAKING THINGS WORSE section of the story. Put another pin here. On to part three: ENDING — AND RECALL.

By the time you're ten years old, you've heard a lot of suspect advice. You know what I mean. Stuff like *If you cross your eyes, they'll stay that way.* Or *You must wait an hour after eating before you go in the pool.* Or *Don't go outside with wet hair.*

I didn't believe any of these life tips. Especially not my uncle's favorite. "Stand up to bullies," he used to say. "Bullies are cowards. If you stand up to them, they'll back down."

Ever try that? I never did. There was a mean guy named Calvin in my class, and I stayed clear of him. I knew as sure as sunrise that if I ever took my uncle's advice and stood up to Calvin, I'd be sitting down really fast with grass stains on my pants.

But this situation was different. My little brother was being bullied. I couldn't let the creep with the tattoos and pierced ears do that to him. I just couldn't.

"Leave him alone!" I shouted.

Of course he didn't back down. He wasn't afraid of me. He walked toward me, pulling my brother after him. My hand hovered over the yellow strip. Did I mean to sound the alarm? Yes. No. Yes and no.

I didn't know what to do.

The metal wheels screeched as we swung around another bend, and fate took the decision out of my hands. I sounded the alarm. I didn't mean to do it, but the car jerked sideways and — as you know — I wasn't good at staying upright without hanging on. My hand flew to the wall to support myself, and I hit the yellow emergency strip by accident.

The creep had even worse balance than I did. He couldn't surf at all. He lost his footing, fell sideways and bashed the side of his head against a pole so hard that he stunned himself and all the earrings on that one ear were torn out. He fell to the floor. The subway pulled into the station and stopped with the doors shut. The cops got there in a few minutes.

And what did they see?

That's right. My little brother in his surfing position in the middle of the subway car, arms out

to balance. Me, on my feet, looking pretty sheepish. And this poor guy — that's how the police saw it — this sad victim on the floor, concussed and bleeding heavily.

Who did they accuse of creating a violent disturbance? Who got in trouble? Who didn't get to eat lunch at Fran's?

And who was laughed at all winter long because of the gigantic purple-and-gold parka his mom bought because he didn't show up at the clothing store on time?

Some days you're a hero and some days you're a clown. This was a clown day.

THE END

I hope you enjoyed that story. If you didn't, too bad, because I'm going to talk about it for a while. We'll discuss the structure and content, and maybe a little about style. Then you can use my story as a model for yours. I want you to imitate it. You find your own voice by imitating someone else's. This isn't illegal or immoral or weird. It's normal. It's how art happens.

CHAPTER 6
WOULD YOU BELIEVE, PIZZA?

Stories are a mix of stuff you know and stuff you make up — truth and lies. In my subway story, the places are real and so are most of the people. But I made up the problem. I cooked up the story from that mix of ingredients. Which leads me to a comparison. An analogy. A way to think about story. The reason I used the word *ingredients* just now is because a story is like . . . a pizza.

Think about it. Pizza is made up of crust, sauce and toppings, which are placed in a hot oven. Crust by itself is not exciting, but you need one. It's the setting of the story. Sauce and toppings give the pizza the flavor you want. They're the characters in your story. After the pizza is prepared, you bake it. The oven is your story problem. Just slide in your setting and characters, and set the dial to WHAT IF.

I set my story on the subway, added myself and my brother and the bully for toppings, and asked a series of *what ifs*: *What if my mouthy brother made the bully mad — and I tried to calm things down by distracting the bully — and it all went wrong — and the bully got hurt — and I got in trouble?*

Follow my recipe to make your story. Let's dive into the details.

CHAPTER 7
CRUST

Setting is where and when your story takes place. Setting grounds your story, gives it stability and a place to grow from. It's important.

Readers want a clear picture of your story world. The more familiar you are with a place, the more confidently you'll be able to describe it and move your characters around within it. That's why your story should be set somewhere you know.

All of my stories are set where I live or where I used to live. I walked and biked through those streets and parks. I hiked those hills. I know them. You can also set your story in an imaginary world *as long as you are totally familiar with it* and can give us clear pictures. Discworld, Rokugan and Wakanda are real places to me because they were real to their creators.

So if you live in Manyberries, Alberta (population 65 when I visited a few years back), by all means set a story there. Ditto Shanghai, China (population 29,211,000 in

2023. I just Googled it.). Or, if you have spent years picturing the licorice fields and coffee rivers of the land of Scrimgeristan (which I just made up), feel free to set your story there. The clearer you see a place in your mind — even a made-up place — the better you'll be able to present it to us so that we can see it too.

But remember this: The places where your story actually takes place — your scene settings — are small. The Simpsons live in the city of Springfield, but the scenes are set in the family living room, Bart's classroom, Mr. Burns's office, etc. Your hero may live in your hometown, but scenes will happen in a classroom or park. A baby sister's day care. A closet where monsters live.

You know those long-distance shots of Earth from space that get clearer and clearer as the camera zooms closer, until we're inside somebody's washing machine and their clothes are getting whiter thanks to a new laundry detergent? Think of your setting like that. My subway story takes place in a city I know well. But notice how detailed my setting is. I zoom in from Toronto → downtown → my house → my living room. That's where my story opens.

Now it's (finally!) time to think about your story. Flex your fingers.

ASSIGNMENT #2: SETTINGS

Maybe you have a clear idea of your story. You *know* it's going to be about that weekend you went camping and got lost, or the time your sister stole your Halloween candy. If so, great! Use this assignment to nail down some of the details.

But maybe you're having trouble coming up with a story idea. Is there a critical voice inside you? Does it boo and hiss and say stuff like *That's a terrible idea! What's wrong with you? You got rocks in your head?* I know that voice.

This assignment can help. I've workshopped it a few times. It's a prompt that lets you sneak up on the story and catch it when it's not looking.

The assignment is in two parts.

1. Write down a few settings for your story. Mine is set in my living room and a subway car. A typical TV sitcom has three or four sets — a living room, an office, maybe a diner. Think of your story like a sitcom. Where does it take place? Your bedroom, the campground, the playground at the park. Good. Now relax. Let your mind go free. Add a few made-up places, even if they seem implausible — a spaceship, a dungeon, a beach on a desert island, the wrong bathroom. Remember to zoom in. Don't just write down *Westeros* or *Vancouver*.

2. Stories move from one setting to another. Work out how your sets go together and think of a title that unites them. It's easy to link, say, your classroom to your school bus to your dining room. You'd call that story "A Day in My Life." Add a cabin on the *Titanic* or an interstellar spaceship, and the story could become "The Day I Time Traveled." Can you link a dungeon, an alien planet and the wrong bathroom? I can. I'll even add creamed corn for dinner in a story called "My Nightmare."

CAN YOU LINK A DUNGEON, AN ALIEN PLANET AND THE WRONG BATHROOM?

You haven't written any of your actual story yet, but you've done some planning. You have a sense of *where* it's taking place. There are other questions to answer before writing that first sentence. So enough about *where*. It's time to think about *who*, in a chapter I call . . .

CHAPTER 8
TOPPINGS

The most important thing about pizza toppings is, well, that we like them. We want to bite into them, engage with them, enjoy them. Same with your characters. If we can't connect with them, we're not going to like your story.

This does NOT mean that every character should be nice and sweet. Who wants a pizza topped with chocolate,

maple syrup, marshmallow, icing sugar and bubble gum? You need a balance. Heroes, villains, tomato sauce, friends, enemies, hot peppers, sidekicks, pets, anchovies.

Anchovies? Really? Super salty little fish?

What can I say? I like them.

Secondary players are important to any story. But they are rarely more important than the main character.

I didn't *start* my subway story with my family or the bad guy. I started with me. And that's what you should do too. You know yourself better than anyone else. So write about yourself. Not that your hero has to *be* you. But they'll think like you, care like you, have your good and bad points. Your main character is the sauce on the pizza, flavoring everything else. The other characters are the rest of the toppings.

If you want to turn yourself into a superhero, fine. But they'll be a cooler version of you. My story has a reluctant hero who gets in trouble. He's like me, for sure. But he's not really me. (If he were really me, he'd grab his little brother and get off the subway car, though he might trip on the way out.)

Who else should be in your story apart from the star? You won't need that many characters. Four or five will carry a TV show through a dozen seasons. Nerdy best friend. Bratty brother. Wise parent. Bossy teacher. Bully. Loser. Cool kid. Goofball.

Or change it up. Bossy parent. Wise best friend. Goofball teacher. Nerdy sister.

Or make your characters animals. Winnie-the-Pooh, Jemima Puddle-Duck, Snoopy and Mr. Toad are completely relatable, aren't they? I have friends and family just like them. (My ex-mother-in-law sounds exactly like Eeyore. Man, she made me laugh!)

You've done a marvelous job so far. And you're going to do even better on the next assignment. Ready? I'll bet you are.

ASSIGNMENT #3: CHARACTERS

We've done an assignment about settings. Let's try one about characters.

The best way to make sure that *readers* care about your characters is for *you* to care about them. Which is easier when you know them. Like the setting, the characters in your story should be familiar to you. They can be based on people you've read about or seen. They can be based on people you know. The thing is, you have to be able to talk about them. My subway story has me, my brother and my mom in it. The guy with the earrings is a bit like Calvin, the boss of my elementary school playground, who made even the teachers nervous.

Like the assignment about settings, this one is in two parts. For the first part, divide a page into two columns — one for people, and the other for their personalities. In other words, WHO YOU KNOW and WHAT THEY'RE LIKE.

I'll go first. Here's mine:

WHO I KNOW	WHAT THEY'RE LIKE
MOM	BOSSY. LOVES TO SAVE MONEY. DOESN'T UNDERSTAND WHY I GET DISTRACTED AND END UP IN TROUBLE. (*PAY ATTENTION, RICHARD!*)
BABA	GREAT COOK. SQUEEZES MY CHEEK AND TELLS ME HOW MUCH SHE LOVES ME. DOESN'T KNOW MUCH ENGLISH, LAUGHS WHEN I TRY TO SPEAK HER LANGUAGE.
CHRISTOPHER	CLASS PRESIDENT, TEAM CAPTAIN, BETTER THAN ME AT EVERYTHING. TALLER, STRONGER, FASTER, SMARTER. WAY CUTER. *SIGH*.
DAVE	LITTLE BROTHER. MOUTHY. FEARLESS. ALWAYS SAYING, "HEY, DID YOU SEE THAT...?"

ZORKA	SUPER POPULAR, SWEARS A LOT. STEALS CANDY. I TRY TO GET HER ATTENTION, BUT SHE IGNORES ME. OH WELL.
CALVIN	STRONG, MEAN, NOT VERY SMART. I'D FEEL SORRY FOR HIM BUT HE'S KIND OF CREEPY. NO ONE LIKES HIM.
CASEY	DARK-HAIRED MUTT. ALWAYS LOOKS LIKE HE'S SMILING. CHASES BALLS, CARS, SQUIRRELS, BUGS, BIRDS, LEAVES, WIND. I GET TIRED JUST WATCHING HIM.

Now you do it. Make a list of seven or eight people you know and what they're like.

OK, that was part one of the assignment. For part two, I want you to mix people and personalities. Draw lines criss-crossing between the two columns. Match a character with someone else's personality. BABA now acts like ZORKA.

Interesting, eh? Imagine what would happen in a story about Thanksgiving dinner, or one about a group science project. . . .

What you're doing here is mixing truth and lies, asking yourself, *What if Baba and Zorka got mixed up? What if my baba was mean and snooty, and my classmate wanted to kiss me and pinch my cheek?!* These would be additions to your story — characters who do not exist in real life.

Which leads us to the next chapter. After *where* and *who*, let's tackle *what* — or, more specifically, *what if*.

CHAPTER 9
OVEN

Settings and characters are lined up. Is it a story? No. You don't eat a pizza until it's baked. That raw dough is bad for you. To say nothing of how the slice falls apart when you try to pick it up, so peppers end up on the floor and you have gunk on your hands and you can't find a napkin, so you lick your fingers or wipe them on your pants, and, well, it's a mess. You don't have pizza without an oven. You don't have a story without a problem.

Most of my story takes place in a subway car. That's my crust. I poured a main character — someone like me — for sauce, and sprinkled three more characters for toppings: brother, mom, bully. But I didn't get a story until I slid everything into the oven of my imagination and set the dial to WHAT IF.

The subway story never happened. I came up with it by taking a normal subway ride with my brother and asking, *What if things were different?*

Is it the only possible story with that setting and those characters? Of course not. That's what's super cool, super fascinating — and super frustrating — about stories. There isn't only one right way to tell them. There isn't only one right answer.

It might be simpler if storytelling was like math or geography. Or riddles. What's 13 × 4? What's the capital of Uruguay? What has four fingers and a thumb but is not alive? There's one correct answer and a universe of incorrect ones.

Telling a story is the reverse. Almost anything might work. My subway bully story could go any number of ways, depending on my choice of *what if*.

What if the old lady stayed on the train, and when the angry tattoo guy threatened my brother, she came over and sprayed him with mace?

What if he was angry because he was cold, and I told him about the sale at Willie's, and he went there with us and found a warm coat?

What if the angry guy came from the future (which would explain his earrings and tattoos), and he and Dave and I went on a time-traveling adventure?

Or, taking a different tack, what if the characters were different? *What if* Dave was a bully picking on some other kid? *What if* he was my dog instead of my brother? *What if* he was blind? Or I was blind, and Dave could be my guide dog?

WHAT IF HE AND DAVE AND I WENT ON A TIME-TRAVELING ADVENTURE?

See what I mean? Super cool, super fascinating . . . and super frustrating. So many things could work. There's one capital of Uruguay. There's one answer to a riddle. (Do you know the one about the fingers and thumb? You don't? Oh.)

Telling a story isn't like solving a riddle. It's like making up a riddle.

ASSIGNMENT #4: PROBLEM

We've done assignments for settings and characters. Let's start thinking about different things that can go wrong. There's a bit of a twist this time. Settings and characters are based on truth. You know the places and people in your story. Problem is different. Problem involves imagination. Remember the pizza analogy. I want you to slide your crust and sauce and toppings into the oven of your imagination, and set the dial to WHAT IF.

This gives us a chance to revisit Assignment #1 — the page divided into six squares, like a comic book, with you filling in a storyboard of what might happen. Remember? Let's do that exercise again, but instead of planning "Hero Meets Dog," make a simple plan for *your* story. You probably want more than one character. You certainly want something to go wrong. If nothing goes wrong, there's no story. How about something like this . . .

YOUR HERO IS SOMEWHERE, AND...	...SOMETHING SURPRISING HAPPENS. WHAT IF YOUR HERO... • MEETS SOMEONE? • LOSES SOMETHING? • FINDS SOMETHING? • GOES SOMEWHERE? • IS THREATENED BY SOMETHING?
YOUR HERO WANTS TO RESOLVE THE SITUATION, SO THEY TRY SOMETHING...	...BUT SOMETHING MAGICAL OR HORRIBLE HAPPENS, WHICH LEADS TO...
...SOMETHING ELSE...	...?

Did you run out of room? Do you want to add another page with another four or six squares? Go for it.

This book is not prescriptive. I don't insist you write THIS way or THAT way any more than I tell you to write about THIS problem or THAT character. I toss a bunch of ideas out there, hoping one of them will appeal to you. If comic book–style storyboarding helps you to come up with a better story, great! If you're still having trouble, don't worry. I have more ideas.

READY TO START?

So far, we've talked (well, I've talked) about looking inside yourself to find something you care about, something that makes you sad or mad or scared. Then I told a story for you to use as a model.

Now, thanks to the assignments, you have some notes:

- Settings you know and can write about

- Characters you know, maybe with some personality crisscrossing

- Ideas of what could go wrong

Prep is almost done. You've planned your story. Now let's talk about the writing itself.

PART 3
WRITING

CHAPTER 10
STYLE

You know the *where*, *who* and *what* of your story. It's time to think about *how* you're going to tell it. I'm talking about style.

Style refers to the *way* you tell the story — the type of writing you use. There are four distinct types of writing. Did you know that? Any phrase in any story will belong to one of those four types. Since you can use any of these types at any point in your story, it makes sense to talk about all of them before you start writing. Here's the start of a story that uses all four of them:

The street was slick after the rain.
A car skidded right at me.
"Help!" I yelled.
I've never been so scared.

Not very good, is it? Sorry about that. But these four sentences illustrate the four essential types of writing, and you'll have to understand them all, even though I'm sure you'll use them to better effect than I just did.

Let's take a look at them in the order I use them.

DESCRIPTION

You want to draw readers into your story. You want them to inhabit this particular piece of your imagination. You want them to see, hear, taste and feel the scene. You want to convey the *atmosphere* of your world. The type of writing that does this most directly is DESCRIPTION.

The street was slick after the rain.

Description is especially useful at the start of a story. We want to know where we are. We want to see it. Are we outside or inside? In a bedroom, in a car, in a classroom, in outer space, in the past, on another planet? Say so. Tell us. Make as clear a picture as you can.

My brother and I were watching TV.

That's OK, but can we make a clearer picture? How about:

My brother and I were watching a row of TVs in Walmart.

Or:

*Take that Saturday morning when I was ten years old,
living downtown, watching cartoons in the living room
with my little brother.*

Description is vital to the setup. Seeing a place or a person helps us to connect with them. Here are a few points to remember about description:

- *You* know the details of your story. You see them in your mind: your living room, your route to school, your mom. It might not occur to you to describe them. But readers have NO IDEA what they look like. Unless you tell us your living room has a swimming pool, or a tiger trap, or a view of the Eiffel Tower, we're going to picture a version of our own living rooms or ones on TV. Do you walk to school past burned-out storefronts? Is your mom a fashion model with an eye patch and a beard? We won't know until you tell us.

  Note: If your living room *does* have a tiger trap in it, don't go into a lot of detail now. Save it for later in the story when the villain falls in. Also remind me not to visit. Also if your mom is a bearded, eye patch–wearing fashion model — super cool!

READERS HAVE NO IDEA WHAT YOUR LIVING ROOM LOOKS LIKE.

- One of the very best ways to describe something is by comparison. Describe it as being *like* something else. That way we get two pictures, and we'll remember the thing better. If you say your aunt's chili tastes like molten lava, we picture a bowl of chili and a volcano. If your aunt's chili tastes like old gym socks, well, we get that picture too. If you say your aunt's chili tastes like a dream of paradise, we get a bunch of pictures, and might hope for a dinner invite.

- Description is pictures, but it's also sounds. And smells. Use all your senses in your descriptions. Ask yourself if the experience is universal or specific. If you open a gym bag (or lunch bag) full of old socks, you don't have to go into too much detail. Just say, "Yuck!" and we'll get it. If your dad singing karaoke sounds exactly like a creaky hinge — or exactly like Cardi B — that's not typical. Tell us.

ACTION

A story that is only a description of someone next to a lamppost sounds pretty boring. Adding more description — moonlight, a distant siren, the taste of chewing gum — isn't going to help much. Sooner or later, something interesting has to happen. We want some ACTION.

A car skidded right at me.

I don't know how much I need to tell you here. Action writing is writing where stuff happens. You know this.

Sometimes the stuff is exciting. Racing or kissing or cartwheeling or eating until you throw up — these are actions. But so is sleeping and sighing and listening to a boring speech.

Getting filthy or frozen, or being threatened by an advancing stream of lava, are actions that happen to you. Washing your hands, putting on a parka or running away are actions you take to deal with your problems.

Whatever your characters are doing, whatever is being done to them — that's action writing. *The creepy guy lurched over to my brother* is an example from my subway story.

Don't worry about putting in *enough* action. Worry about making it interesting. Here are a couple of things to think about:

- Mix up the pace. Don't have everything happen *Pow! Zap! Run! Escape-just-in-time!* Calmer moments give readers a chance to relax in between bouts of excitement. Change it up. DJs plan their whole set in advance. They want the tracks to flow together, building and releasing suspense, keeping the audience engaged for an hour or more at a time. Plan your story like a DJ.

- Think *because*, not *and then*. Dave and I were on the subway because we were meeting Mom because she had found a sale. I challenged the stranger because he was threatening Dave. The stranger fell because he wasn't used to subway surfing. His car was bleeding because his piercings were torn out. The events may be ridiculous, but they hang together better because of all the *becauses*. We'd have trouble believing a series of unrelated events. *I fell down the stairs, then there was a power outage, then the aliens landed, then I turned into a giant carrot, then I threw up all over the Taj Mahal, then I woke up and it was all a dream. . . .* Lousy story, right?

THEN I TURNED INTO A GIANT CARROT . . .

DIALOGUE

Narrating events is telling your readers what happened: *Once upon a time there was a king who lived in a rainy country. . . . A family of three bears lived in a cottage in the forest. . . . A miller had three sons. . . .* And so on.

Here's the start of my subway story in narrative:

> *My brother and I went to buy winter coats. Trouble started when a stranger got on our subway car. . . .*

Narrative moves your story along briskly. Pausing the narrative and adding DIALOGUE — letting your characters talk — creates a scene.

> *"Help!" I yelled.*

I was going to talk about this later, but since we're here, and since understanding scene and narrative are basic to story writing, let's do it now.

You've probably heard the phrase "show, don't tell." Maybe your teacher says it. Narration is telling. Scenes are showing. Scenes are the parts of the story where characters are in the same time and place, talking to each other. Here, for instance, is the start of a scene:

"I think Darleen likes you," I whispered to my friend Sanjay. We sit together at the back of science class.

"What?" He dropped his pencil in surprise. "Darleen?"

The teacher stopped talking about the water cycle and frowned at us.

"What is going on back there?" she asked in a voice that would curdle milk.

Scenes happen in a particular moment. You can use narration instead of scene to move faster. Or use narration to link scenes together. For instance:

In science class, I told my pal Sanjay that Darleen liked him. Two periods later, we were sitting at our usual lunch table, when Darleen came over. And you'll never guess what happened then.

The first sentence of this narration paragraph could take the place of the scene in science class. Or, if you prefer, you can keep the scene with you and your friend and the teacher's curdled milk voice, and use narration to get you both to the cafeteria. Darleen comes over, and I guess we're getting ready for another scene where she says something mean to Sanjay, or kisses him, or whatever.

I'll have a little more to say about scene and narration when we get to the rewrite section of the book. "Show, don't tell" is good advice, but you don't have to follow it blindly. It's a kindness to help old people across the street, but that doesn't mean you should grab everyone with white hair and drag them into traffic.

Back to dialogue. It's probably my favorite kind of writing. When you're reading, do you skip over some descriptions? Say there's a page-long paragraph describing the sky, or someone's clothes, or the front of a house — do you skim over that? Of course you do. We all do. But you don't skip the dialogue.

Let's get technical for a minute. Do you know what an "inquit phrase" is? No? OK. It's a short phrase attached to direct speech to let the reader know who's talking. *He said* is an inquit phrase. So are *she asked* and *they wondered*. Inquit phrases are also called "dialogue tags." You don't always have to use them. Here are a boy and his mom. You know who's saying what, even without dialogue tags.

"This room looks like a pigsty, Steve."
　"Aw, Ma."
　"Tidy it at once."
　"But the guys and I are going to go to —"
　"At once, I said!"

In a more confusing conversation, inquit phrases help readers know what's going on. Here's a hint: By far the most common phrase — the one that sounds most natural — the best one — is *said*. We are so used to reading the word *said* that we ignore it and focus on the speech itself. If you use an unlikely synonym for *said*, and have your characters *expostulating* or *opining* or *asseverating* all over the place, we'll get distracted.

I'm not saying you should only use *said*. Sometimes a character is upset or is asking a question. My example at the start of this chapter has the narrator yelling, "Help!" In the subway story, I whisper a couple of times. But *said* should be your go-to.

No matter what you do about inquit phrases, you can switch up your presentation. Here's the messy room scene with a few different dialogue possibilities:

"Could you please clean your room, Steve?" asked his mom.

"But I don't want to," he said.

"Please!" she repeated, not like a request. It was more like an order.

"You can't make me." He was pouting now.

"Do it," she said, "or you won't go to the dance tomorrow night."

"Mom!"

You can use dialogue for all kinds of things. Dialogue can move the action forward. Like this:

"Where are you going with that razor?" I asked Jorrin.

"I want to shave the rottweiler next door," he said.

"What? Rex is chained up because he bit someone. He's dangerous."

"Don't worry, this is a safety razor. Nothing can go wrong."

Or:

"What's that in your coat pocket?" I asked Jorrin.

"Nothing. Shhhh!"

"Is it a candy bar? Are you trying to steal a candy bar? What if the store guy sees us? He's staring at us now!"

"SHHHH!"

Dialogue is also great for revealing character or relationship. Like this:

"Chicken for lunch again today, Jorrin?"

"Duh! Read the letters on the box. What do you think the C stands for — corn? You think this is Kentucky Fried Corn?"

"I was just making conversation."

"Stupid is what you were making. You were making stupid."

Or:

"Why are you sighing?" I asked.

"Because I love you," said Jorrin. "Do you love me too?"

"Uhh," I said.

"Say it. Say you love me too."

"Uhhhhhhhh," I said.

(Does Jorrin remind you of anyone you know? I sure hope not.)

More than any other kind of writing, dialogue tests your connection with the reader. You must make your characters sound convincing. Description is easier. It's your world, so we'll believe whatever you tell us. If you describe a green sky with two suns, we'll believe it. If you tell us your hero's grandma is a nunchuck champion who works as a bouncer at a biker bar, we'll believe you. Weird but cool, we'll think. Good for Grandma. But we're not going to believe unconvincing dialogue like this:

"Oh my," said Grandma to the biker. "That is a bad thing you are doing."

"Is it indeed a bad thing?" said the biker.

"Yes. Yes, it is a bad thing," said Grandma. "It is such a bad thing that you should stop doing it."

"All right then," said the biker. "I will stop doing the bad thing."

You don't have to make your characters into stereotypes to be believable. Grandma doesn't have to have white hair and old-timey clothes and a smile for everyone. She can wear a leather jacket or a scuba suit. She can be super mean. In the same way, the biker can be pleasant and shy. But the characters should *sound* believable. They should sound like people talking, not reading from cue cards or practicing a foreign language.

Also, they shouldn't sound the same. If your gran and your bus driver, and the class bully and the class nerd, and the old guy at the pet store and your friend's baby brother — if all these characters sound the same — that's not good dialogue.

This book focuses on what I like about story. It's not a grammar book. I'm not going to deal with punctuation, except for this short section here. I include it because most of the grammar mistakes I see involve dialogue writing.

Punctuation isn't the most important part of a story, but you notice it. Think of it like hygiene. Being clean isn't as important as being healthy. It's not as important as being nice. But filthy is not your best look. No matter how charming you are, it's hard to make friends at the party if you show up with mud on your jeans and snot on your face. In a story, good punctuation is less important than memorable characters or a gripping problem. But bad punctuation is distracting.

And it's easy to fix. Read almost any published story or article with dialogue and make your punctuation look like that. One and done.

Check the exchanges in this chapter. They're all OK.

REVIEW: DESCRIPTION, ACTION AND DIALOGUE

Were you paying attention over the last few pages? I'll set up our review as a Q and A.

WHAT IS THE VALUE OF GOOD *DESCRIPTION*?

It brings us into the story. We know the shape of the landscape, what the hero is wearing, what the villain's smile is reminiscent of, and so on. The tone of the description is a large part of the atmosphere.

SHOULD *ACTION* BE FAST-PACED OR SLOW-PACED?

Both. Slow to build tension, then fast to release it. For example:

> *Jess took a step forward, and another one, and a third. She reached for the doorknob, turning it slowly, carefully. The door creaked as it opened and —*
>
> *The Bandersnatch leaped at her with a frumious roar. Jess ran.*

IS THERE ANYTHING YOU CAN'T DO WITH *DIALOGUE*?

"I'll let this answer speak for itself."

THAT'S ONLY THREE TYPES OF WRITING. WHAT'S THE FOURTH TYPE?

Glad you asked.

INSIGHT

The fourth kind of writing is what I call INSIGHT. You could also call it *feeling* or *emotion* or *observation* or *perception*. This kind of writing shows us what a character is thinking or feeling. In the story template I gave you at the beginning of the chapter, the narrator has never been so scared.

I've never been so scared.

Different kinds of writing offer different ways of connecting with readers. And connecting, as I've said a bunch of times, is the main task of a story creator. If you don't connect, you can't get anyone to turn the page. Which means you can't inform anyone. You can't amuse or persuade anyone. You can't make anyone laugh or cry or care.

Insight is the most direct kind of connection. It's inside information. The narrator is either talking directly to us or giving us a chance to eavesdrop on characters. This is the truth as far as that character knows it.

Let's look again (I know, I know) at the subway story.

There isn't much description: living room, subway car. The only detailed picture is the stranger, since he's a bit different from what you might think, and without him there's no story. Action? Sure. Dave and I do things, and things happen to us. Dialogue moves the plot along and gives a sense of the characters. You know more about Dave and Mom and the bully from the way they talk.

Which brings us to insight. There's a lot of it in the story. I start and finish by talking directly to readers:

You're always the star of your own life . . . This was a clown day.

I go on about the dumb advice adults give to kids. That's one kind of insight: what the author is thinking. Another kind tells readers how characters feel, either directly:

Dave wasn't scared at all. I was.

Or indirectly:

Oh no. Oh no oh no oh no!

These insights get to the motivations behind the story: why characters act the way they do.

So, the first sentence in my story is a piece of insight. There's more insight in the first paragraph. Also the third, fifth, sixth, eighth, tenth, twelfth . . . OK, I stopped counting. There's a lot of insight. Did I say I liked dialogue best? Maybe I was lying.

There's lots of insight in films or plays. Anytime you hear the narrator talking to you in what the screenplay calls voice-over, that's insight. Shakespeare's soliloquies are insight. "To be or not to be . . ." — that's Hamlet talking to the audience. There's no one else onstage.

Insight is time away from the story. You're pushing the PAUSE button on your plot in order to talk to readers. You don't want them to lose interest, so don't take too long. Just because something in the story reminds you of something your aunt said at Thanksgiving dinner, which made your mom so mad she called your aunt a bad word, which made you laugh so hard you choked on the Swiss chard, which your dad had sautéed with tarragon to cut the bitterness, because he was sick of people complaining about the . . . Wait, I got lost.

See what happens?

Insight can bring readers closer to the characters but further from the storyline. Be careful of using too much. I'm going to suggest that you keep the plot moving. My editor often tells me this. In fact, she's telling me this right now.

CHAPTER 11

TIME TO START

No more prep. No more pizza. No more scales. No more wax on, wax off. Assignment #5, at the end of this chapter, is to write the opening section of your story. We're going to divide your story into three pieces.

(*Like pizza slices?* Enough with the pizza, Richard.)

You can think of them as beginning, middle and end, because that's where they show up. We'll talk about the sections one at a time, because that's how you'll write your story.

The beginning is the setup. This is where you establish your story world's look and feel, the rules and boundaries.

Help your readers. You want them intrigued (*I wonder what'll happen next?*) but not too confused (*Huh? I'm so lost I give up.*). Your opening section should describe the location, introduce the characters and get them into trouble. It should answer the questions we have at the start of any story: Where are we? Who should we care about? What's wrong?

Think about these questions when you write your setup.

Where?

Who?

What's wrong?

In my model story, the setup takes Dave and me from our living room to the subway car. We're in a hurry. We want to meet Mom so we can get parkas that fit and lunch at a restaurant. Onto our car walks a strange guy.

That's it. Where, who, what's wrong.

Setup doesn't have to take long. One of my favorite picture books opens with a little girl in bed, wearing a puzzled expression and . . . well, here's the opening sentence:

> *On Thursday, when Imogene woke up, she found she had grown antlers.*

That's a solid setup right there. Where, who and what's wrong all at once.

My subway story fills about five pages. That's the length of story you're probably going to write. The setup takes about a third of that. Page and a half, maybe a bit less. Five hundred words or so. Think about those first five hundred words. Writing them is going to be your next assignment.

I have one last thing to say about setup. You should start your story *when the story starts.* That sounds obvious, but it's not. *Imogene's Antlers* doesn't start when she goes to bed looking like a normal girl. It starts when she wakes up with antlers on her head.

My subway story doesn't start with me and Dave getting up, pouring cereal for breakfast, saying goodbye to Mom, dashing to the living room in our flannel pajamas. (Mine were yellow, his were green.) I don't spend a page or two commenting on the cartoons we watched — Daffy and Dastardly and Bullwinkle and the rest. The story is not about these things. The story is about me and Dave getting in trouble on the subway, so I move us there pretty quickly.

I have written over twenty books, which means over twenty first drafts, and in almost every one of those first drafts, I started too early. Fortunately, I remember a piece of advice from Paul, one of my writing instructors. "When you've finished the first few pages," he said, "go back and take out the opening paragraph. Paragraph two or three is where your story really starts."

I've taken Paul's advice with every story and novel I've written. Amazing how often he was right. You can use this advice too. Ask yourself why the story is starting *now*? Why not yesterday or tomorrow or next week? What's different about this moment?

After all these pages, I hope you understand the importance of planning your story. Enough already! (One of my mom's favorite phrases.) Enough planning. It's time to get out whatever you write with — pen and paper, keyboard, crayon, India ink, blood of your mortal enemies — and write a page or two. That's all the space you need to introduce your setting and main characters and get to the point where they run into a problem. Feel free to use any or all of the four types of writing in your setup. But make sure there is at least some description. We want to see where we are.

Start your story, and write until you reach the point where your readers are going to think *Oh, oh!* Then stop.

If you have an idea for where the story is going to go, great. If you don't, that's OK too. I'm here for you. We'll go through the next stages of the story together and gather some ideas as we go.

... PEN AND PAPER, CRAYON, INDIA INK, BLOOD OF YOUR MORTAL ENEMIES ...

Not so fast. We're due for a quiz, don't you think?

No? Tough.

The questions are designed to test what you know and also to hint at what's coming up. It's a quiz you'll learn from as you write it. Not bad, eh? And the answers are right after, in case you get confused.

QUIZ

1. A story opens with a girl walking down the street. How many of these *what if* ideas can work? *What if . . .*

   a) she finds a gemstone of power?

   b) she meets a stranger who makes her a surprising offer?

   c) she has a giant sneezing fit and runs out of tissues?

d) she yawns so wide she dislocates her jaw?

e) she gets kidnapped by mobsters who demand ransom money from her megarich parents?

f) she gets to school, spends the day there, goes home, has a snack, does her homework, plays games on her phone, has dinner with her family, goes to bed, and wakes up to find that she has turned into a giant cockroach?

2. A story opens with a rock and a pair of scissors walking down the street. Can this storyline work? How would you continue?

3. A story opens in a classroom. The teacher is taking attendance. How many of the twenty-five students do we care about?

4. A story opens with *It was a day like any other day. . . .* Now what?

ANSWERS TO QUIZ

1. ALL of the ideas can work. But the last idea (f) needs to be changed so that the story starts later on, with our hero waking up. Remember, start your story where the story starts.

2. Of course the story can work. Rock and Scissors get into an argument about sports or fast food, and Rock *crushes* Scissors. Then Paper comes along and *covers* Rock. Scissors climbs shakily to her feet and *cuts* Paper. They are all late for school.

3. We will not be able to keep twenty-five students straight in our minds. A short story is going to be about a smaller cast of characters. Maybe three of the girls are named Megan. Megan Glasses, Megan Braids, Megan I've-Got-A-Better-Idea. The opening

scene has the teacher assigning them a group project. Things go wrong when we meet a mischievous little brother named Oryx.

4. Rip up the page. Or, if the story is on the computer, roll your eyes and say, loudly, "Wow, what a boring opening!" as you delete the file. Remember, stories are about days that are different from other days. That's why they are worth writing about.

Congratulations. You all did really well on the quiz. You get stickers. Seriously now, are you ready to move on? Are you sure? There's no rush. I have nothing to do. I can wait here all day.

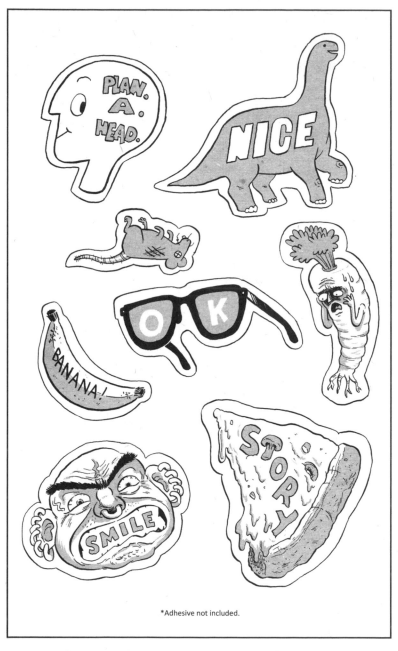

*Adhesive not included.

YOU ALL DID REALLY WELL ON THE QUIZ. YOU GET STICKERS.

ASSIGNMENT #5: THE BEGINNING

This is the bit where you do Assignment #5. Write your opening section.

Ready . . . (take a last slurp of whatever you drink) . . .

Set . . . (phone off) . . .

Go — (what's that? You're already typing? All right, I'll shut up.)

THIS READER IS DOING ASSIGNMENT #5. NOTICE THE DEEP CONCENTRATION!

NO PHONE, NO FOOD, NO DISTRACTIONS. I WISH I WAS THAT FOCUSED.

Finished so soon? Outstanding! Next topic is the middle section of the story, which I call . . .

CHAPTER 12

MAKING THINGS WORSE

This is the section where you address the problem you introduced in your setup. When I say address, I do not mean fix. Do not solve your problem. In fact, I suggest that you MAKE THINGS WORSE.

In the setup of my subway story, the bully gets on. By the end of the second section, he's attacking my brother, and I'm threatening to stop the subway. Things are definitely worse.

This is how any middle section works. In *Fantasia*, Mickey Mouse has a problem when the sorcerer's broom won't follow orders. What happens? One broom becomes a handful of brooms, a dozen brooms, an army of brooms! Dorothy Gale runs away from mean Almira Gulch in the setup to *The Wizard of Oz*. In the middle section, Dorothy must deal with a nastier version of Almira as the Wicked Witch of the West. Every video game gets harder as you play. *Super Mario Odyssey* takes you from planet to planet, battling increasingly powerful bosses. *Portal* starts in a science lab with Chell taking tests that become more and more (and more!) hazardous.

Whatever the problem in your setup, make *more* of it in the middle section. Let's say your story opens with your hero spilling something on their jeans. In the middle section of that story, the liquid soaks through and burns their leg. They have to run to the bathroom to take off their jeans, but the fire alarm rings and . . . well, you get the idea.

Here are a couple of things to be thinking of while you write your middle section:

1. *Don't use too many eggs.* The British have some unique expressions. If you're upset, they'll say you're "throwing a wobbly." And if you're trying too hard to improve

something, they'll warn you against "over-egging the pudding." Remember that advice when you're writing your middle section. One complication is good, but two is not twice as good, and three or four is certainly too many. You may be tempted to make your problem worse, then worse again, and then even worse than that. Resist that temptation. My story would *not* be better if eight more large scary guys got on at the next stop, took over the train, held us hostage, and jammed the steering so that the train jumped the track at Union Station and crashed through the retaining wall into Lake Ontario, where it filled with water and sank through a portal in the lake bottom, transporting us all to another universe, where sheets of fire fell like rain and humans wore asbestos umbrellas on their heads. (Mind you, in this universe Dave and I would not need winter coats.)

Seriously, keep your middle section focused. Make the problem worse *once*. If your hero throws a wobbly, that's fine. But don't over-egg the pudding.

2. *Keep problems consistent with character.* My brother gets in trouble because he's mouthy and fearless. That's who Dave was — that's who he is now. (He's a trial lawyer. Say no more.) Later, the problem gets worse when

I lose my balance and hit the emergency strip by accident. That clumsy goofball was (and, yes, still is) me. If your hero is graceful and athletic, the problem should not be that they stumble. If they are super tall, maybe they bump into a chandelier. If they have a loud voice, maybe the wrong person overhears them.

3. *Add a new character.* This is not a hard-and-fast rule, but it's something to think about. A new character can threaten your hero in a surprising way. Which means your new character should be different from your other ones. If you have a hero and a sidekick and a villain, don't add another sidekick. Maybe your new character could be a baby. Or a dog. Or a wizard. Or a baby dog wizard.

ASSIGNMENT #6: THE MIDDLE

The middle section is usually a bit longer than the opening. If your setup was a couple pages long, aim for almost double that for the middle. Don't worry if you don't have an ending yet. We'll talk about finishing your story over the next few chapters.

You probably want to focus less on description in the middle than you did in the opening. We know now what your world and your hero look like. This is a busy section. Things happen. Make sure there's plenty of action and dialogue.

Get writing, already! Don't move on until you've made your story problem worse.

CHAPTER 13

END WITH A BACKWARD LOOK

You've set up your story. You've made things worse. Now you're ready to finish.

How do you do it? How do you bring the story home?

Good news: you only need to write another couple of pages.

More good news: Ending a story is easier than starting one. When you start a story, the page is blank. You can write about whatever you want — a stranded whale, a goalie on the Slovenian national ice hockey team, two teens meeting on the dance floor, a stuffed dog that goes on a trip. Anything is possible.

Every choice removes possibilities. When you decide on a teen romance, you eliminate the stranded whale and runaway stuffie. As you make things worse for your romantic characters (parents and friends don't get along, there's a duel, a death, a magic potion — you know, the usual), the way ahead gets even narrower. By the time we get near the end — about where you are in your story

A STORY ABOUT ROMANCE CUTS OUT THE RUNAWAY STUFFED ANIMAL.

now — there are basically only two choices. Either they get together or they don't.

Either ending can work. But those are the only two endings. You can't end your love story with a tidal wave that saves a stranded whale or with a Slovenian goalie stopping a breakaway. Stories end by addressing the key problem.

Think of a favorite song. How does the song end? It doesn't leave you hanging in midair, does it? It might end with a big bang, or a gradual fadeaway, but it won't just stop. A scale doesn't go *do re mi fa so la ti*. It ends where it started, on *do*.

It's the same with story. When a story ends well, you are satisfied. Whether the ending is happy or sad, some kind of right thing has happened. After a long journey, you have arrived at a new place that recalls the place where you began. You have come back to *do*.

My subway story ends unhappily. I'm late meeting my mom because I'm talking to the cops, and end up with a parka way too big for me. That's the last thing I talk about.

Do I mention the coat earlier in the story?

Why yes. Yes I do. It's the reason Dave and I were on the subway in the first place. Referring back to the coat is my way of tying the end of the story to the beginning. You grab readers' attention by using a *story hook*. You let

go by using what I call a *hook back*. The backward look — the hook back — brings the story home, completes the scale and brings us back to *do*.

Hook backs have been around forever. At the end of every story, there's a reference to an earlier part. So when you're finishing off your story, make sure to draw our attention backward.

This is not a trick or hack — this is standard story practice. This is like washing your hands, stopping at a red light, saying please and thank you.

I have something important to say about where hook backs come from. The best way to make my point is to demonstrate, so I'm going to tell another story. You must be sick of that subway one by now anyway.

CHAPTER 14
"SAVING SUSIE"

When I was nine years old, I lived in a subdivision in a suburb of Toronto. I came home from school one sunny September afternoon and, since there was nothing on TV, I went to the kitchen to make myself a peanut butter sandwich.

(Pay attention to that peanut butter sandwich. It's important.)

I was spreading peanut butter *(crunchy peanut butter — the best kind. Don't forget!)* when I heard very faintly, in the background, a siren. I shrugged and went back to the peanut butter sandwich *(which you're not forgetting, right?)*. But the siren got louder, louder, LOUDER!

I put down my sandwich and went to the front window as a fire engine roared past, bells clanging, siren blaring, firefighters hanging on for dear life. I jumped on my bike and followed the fire engine around a couple of corners. It stopped in front of a huge fire. I stared because the fire was at my friend Billy's house!

Billy was sitting on the lawn, crying. I told him how sorry I was about his house, and he sniffed and nodded — and that's when I noticed that his little sister, Susie, wasn't with him. Susie was maybe three years old, had curly dark hair and big black eyes, and back then she talked with a lisp. Like *thith*. When she said her own name, it came out sounding like *Thuthie*. OK?

I couldn't see Billy's sister until I checked the house itself. And there in the living room window, I saw the top half of a curly dark head. That's right. Little Susie was trapped in the burning house!

The firefighters were still getting their hoses ready. The front door was open. Before I knew it, I was dashing up the walk and slipping into the house. There were no flames downstairs, but the front hall was full of smoke. I covered my face with my sleeve and coughed my way into the living room. Little Susie was trapped behind the couch. I picked her up and carried her out just as the firefighters were rushing in. They got us outside, gave us oxygen, and we were fine. They yelled at me for putting my life in danger, but everyone else thought I was a hero.

Billy and I took Susie for a walk a couple days later. We each held one of her hands so she wouldn't fall. At the end of our street was a main road with a bus route. There was a paving crew at work.

"Whatth that?" Susie lisped. She pulled free of our hands to point at the big yellow machine. Of course she stumbled off the sidewalk onto the road. And at just that moment, a little red Hyundai turned into the subdivision, and —

What do you think happened?

This is how I tell the story when I'm visiting a school. I'll be in the gym in front of a hundred kids, and I'll get this far in the story and stop.

"What do you think happened?" I ask. "There's no right answer. The story ends however you want it to."

The kids shout out a bunch of different ideas. It's like I made the pizza and put it in the oven, and they decide when it's done. Take it out or leave it in? Turn up the heat?

I have heard some hilarious endings. One audience had a giant eagle swoop down and carry Susie off before the car hit her. The eagle took her to my place and dropped her onto the trampoline in my backyard. Another group of students had me dash into the road to save Susie again. In this version, her mom was so grateful that she bought me a big bag of candy. I like that version a lot.

Some audiences don't want a happy ending. One version has Susie run over by the car and walking with a limp for the rest of her life. Other versions are even more gruesome than that.

Here's one of my favorites. I borrowed it from an elementary school in Cobourg, Ontario, and adapted it for this chapter. Ready?

. . . And at just that moment, a little red Hyundai turned into the subdivision, and ran right over Susie, crushing her flat. The driver pulled over to the curb in horror and looked back at the little body lying right in the path of an oncoming bus.

Yes, the big road was a bus route. The driver saw poor Susie lying there and slammed on the brakes. Too late. The bus couldn't stop in time. It ran over what was left of Susie, crushing her even flatter. And then . . .

Remember the big yellow machine she had pointed at? They were paving the road, right? Well, she was pointing at a steamroller. And now it was rolling right toward her body. The driver hauled on the hand brake. Could he stop in time?

Nope. Oh dear. Poor little Susie was — GULP — spread all over the intersection, *just like the peanut butter on my sandwich at the beginning of this story.*

Now you know why I told you to pay attention to it.

POOR LITTLE SUSIE WAS SPREAD ALL OVER THE INTERSECTION . . .

CHAPTER 15

HOOKS

When the crowd decides that Susie should die, there are gasps and giggles. It's surprising. It's grisly. And it's funny. People like grisly and funny. I tell them not to worry about Susie, because she'll live again every time the story is told. THAT is the power of story. Cartoons have always known this. Wile E. Coyote sets ridiculous traps for the Road Runner and gets flattened or blown up or hurled into space. Three seconds later, he's back and scheming. Singed, sliced, squashed, smithereened, Coyote lives on.

The point of telling the Susie story in this book is the ending, the recall of the peanut butter sandwich. One of the most common story endings is a link back to the beginning of the story. The peanut butter sandwich is a *hook back*.

Let's talk some more about them.

The gruesome kids in Cobourg decided that the story would end with Susie doing badly — one of the two possible places for the plot to go. But they did not come up with the peanut butter sandwich. That was me, the storyteller. The idea of the poor girl spread across the intersection made me think of other things you spread — like peanut butter. I revisited the opening of the story and added the peanut butter sandwich. Now the ending of the story links back to the start.

Do you see?

Different endings would require different hook backs. Remember the version where I save Susie and her mom gives me a candy reward? For that ending, I'd change the story opener. No peanut butter sandwich. This time, I'd wish for a candy bar on the way home from school. I'd search the kitchen for a candy bar. *Oh, if only I had a candy bar!*

In the version where the eagle swoops down just in time and carries Susie away, the start of the story would have me notice an eagle perched on a telephone pole on my way home from school. *What a huge bird!* I'd think. *It's almost big enough to lift me.* Maybe I'd see the bird again, circling high over Billy's house.

Hook backs are often created back to front. After you finish your story, go back and add something to the start that links to the ending. Now it reads as if you planned it that way.

It's an illusion.

———

Some of the most famous hook backs involve revealing something that has been true all along. Alice wakes up from Wonderland and says, "I've had such a curious dream!" Max, alone and hungry, goes to where the wild things are and gets back in time for dinner.

Bookending is a common kind of hook back. Start the story after the adventure is over and you're in the hospital (or having dinner, or winning that award), then go back and tell us how you got to where your story started.

ASSIGNMENT #7: THE END

OK, it's time to finish off your story. This is where you write the last couple of pages. Your hook back will probably have something to do with *why* your hero is on their quest, what they *want*. That's what the story is about, after all. Go back to your opening paragraphs and set that hook.

Please feel free to use all four types of writing, but the bring-it-home section of the story is often a good time for insight. Your hero can think meaningful thoughts or address the reader, giving us something to take away from the story. *The real peanut butter sandwich is the friends we made along the way*, or whatever.

Away you go. I'll do something else while I'm waiting for you to finish.

Can't think of anything? Here's a simple trick: Reach into your pocket right now. Take the pen, loose change, button or whatever you found, and add it to your story. (Maybe your hero writes the life-changing phone number with the pen.) Set the story hook in the first paragraph when you put the thing in your hero's pocket, then hook back at the end.

I've used this trick myself. Years ago, I was writing a story about getting lost on a camping trip. I found a paper clip in my pocket, and it gave me the idea to have my hero improvise a fishhook.

IT GAVE ME THE IDEA TO HAVE MY HERO IMPROVISE A FISHHOOK.

CHAPTER 16
REVIEW

If you've skimmed up until now, here's your chance to catch up. I'll set it up like another Q and A. From the beginning. . . .

WHAT IS A STORY?

An account or telling of events. Something happens.

ARE STORIES TRUE?

Yes. And no. All stories have truth in them. This book is about writing fiction, which usually starts with truth but also includes lies to make the story more interesting.

WHAT DOES A STORY NEED TO HAVE?

Setting, characters, problem.

ARE THERE ANY RULES TO TELLING A GOOD STORY?

No.

NO RULES AT ALL?

All right, there's one rule: Make it interesting. Readers should want to read on.

CAN I COMPARE STORY TO SOMETHING ELSE?

You can think of a story lots of different ways. A story is something you build up from the ground, like a snowman or a sandcastle or a mud pie. It's something that hits you from the sky, like a raindrop or a sunbeam or a bolt of lightning. It's something you put together from connecting pieces, like a jigsaw puzzle. A story is like a game you play, or a journey you take, or an illness you suffer. A story is like being born, or dying, or falling in love, or going to the bathroom. You can compare story to anything. It's life.

HOW ABOUT A USEFUL COMPARISON?

In this book, I compare story to a pizza.

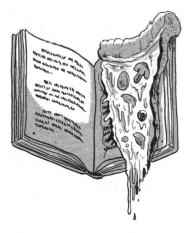

GO ON . . .

To make pizza, you add toppings to a crust and throw it into an oven. For a story, you add characters to a setting and throw it into your imagination.

WHICH PARTS OF A STORY ARE REAL AND WHICH ARE MADE UP?

The setting is a place you know well — either because you live there or because you dream about it all the time. It's real for you. The characters are real too — or based on real people. Your mom, your dog, your friend Spencer. You. The story problem is made up.

HOW DO I START MY STORY?

I'd start with the setup — establishing where we are and getting your main character into trouble. But there are no rules. If you want to write the ending first, do that.

DO I HAVE TO KNOW HOW MY STORY ENDS BEFORE I START?

Nope. All you need to start is a setting and a hero and an idea of what might go wrong. Write your setup, then make things worse, and *then* wonder how to hook it back and bring it home. You'll know how the story ends when you're done.

WHAT SHOULD I DO IF I CAN'T THINK OF A STORY IDEA?

The best story-building emotions are fear, sadness and anger. For a hack or shortcut to your story, think of a moment when you were truly scared, sad or mad. Then twist that moment by asking yourself, *What if things were different? What if something terrible happened? What if that creepy doll came to life and tried to kill you?* Or *What if something magical happened? What if you closed your eyes and vanished?*

WHAT KINDS OF FICTION WRITING ARE THERE?

Novels and short stories, poetry and screenplays and plays. These are all fiction. So are comics and graphic novels and picture books. Story writing for video games is fiction too. So is a note saying you were in bed with the flu yesterday, or that you'll be home by 9:00 p.m., but we don't have to go there.

I MEAN DIFFERENT TYPES OF WRITING IN FICTION.

People talk about literary fiction, where realistic problems — getting sick, losing money — happen to people like you. This is supposed to be different from *genre* fiction, where the problems are larger than life and the characters might be superheroes or aliens. Mystery, romance, science fiction and fantasy are considered to be genre fiction. Of course, there's lots of crossover. Real-life stories can be mysteries. Or romances. There's also a difference between writing for children and writing for adults, though again there are lots of crossovers.

NO, NO! WHAT KIND OF WRITING SHOULD I USE? WHAT SHOULD MY PAGE LOOK LIKE?

Ohhhhhhh. I see. Sorry. There are four basic styles of writing that go into a story. *Description* paints pictures of the scene or the characters. *Action* tells us what is going on. *Dialogue* is conversation between characters. *Insight* is writing from inside the narrator's head and heart, pausing the action to show us what they are thinking about or how they feel. You don't need all four styles on every page, but you probably want to use them all.

WHEN I ADD A STORY HOOK TO LINK THE BACK OF MY STORY TO THE FRONT, AM I DONE?

Nope. Not you, not me, not [insert your favorite author's name here]. No matter how successful you are, you don't get everything in your story right the first time. See how many pages are left in this book?

PART 4
REWRITING

CHAPTER 17
WHAT IS A REWRITE?

So you've finished your story!

You did all the things we've talked about. You took characters based on you and the people you know, placed them in a setting you describe in clear detail and gave them a problem. You made things worse, then found an ending that linked back to an earlier part of the story.

Your prose includes description, action, dialogue and insight. Your pizza has a solid crust, tasty toppings and it's perfectly cooked. You're done, right?

Nope.

Art is failure, said Samuel Beckett in one of his optimistic moods. He didn't mean that all art stinks. What he was getting at is that you'll never be able to say exactly what you want. There is no such thing as a perfect story any more than there is a perfect statue or a perfect song (though "Itsy Bitsy Spider" comes close).

You don't get it right the first time. This is certainly true when you are starting out. Even a canny old codger like me, who has published a bunch of books, doesn't nail a story right away. Every single book I have written has gone through multiple drafts. Every. Single. Book. Including this one. The sentence you're reading now is different than it was when I first wrote it. (How's that for meta!)

Rewriting means more than checking your spelling and grammar. Rewriting means taking your story apart, checking the soundness of the most important pieces, and then putting your story back together. Over the next few chapters, I'll discuss what your plot and characters should have going for them. I'll also talk about word choices for the first time. I've avoided that aspect of style until now because it's a personal part of writing, and because I don't know how teachable it is. But it relates to qualities I mention a lot. Is the story interesting? Is the reader engaged? Do we want to turn the page? Writing style is an important part of a story's success, and the rewrite is the time to tackle it.

We'll look at the rewrite process in detail. Plot first.

CHAPTER 18
PLOT CHECKLIST

Your story should involve conflict, something going wrong. (Remember? We talked about this.) When you're checking over your plot, note that conflict is not a straight line: A versus B. Conflict is shaped like a triangle: A versus B in order to achieve C. The hero's struggle against the raging flood also involves saving the village. A fight between rival gangs (or nations or planets) pits the two sides against

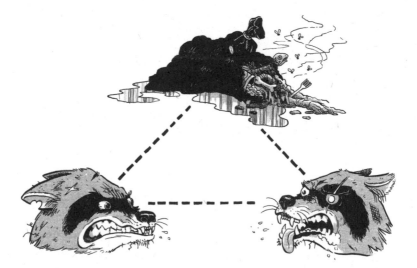

each other in order to obtain neighborhood control (or mineral rights or galactic dominance, or whatever). A duel will be *about* something: honor, love, a secret. The village safety, or neighborhood control, or love interest — that's the third corner of the triangle. When you're checking the conflict in your story, do not lose sight of that third corner. Remind us what the stakes are.

Do you want to broaden or deepen the conflict in your plot? I haven't talked much about *secrets* yet. Let's do it now. A secret is something that not everyone knows. Makes sense, right? One kind of secret is a mystery. There's a dead body or missing will or lost dog, and *no one* knows who did it, or where it is. Not the hero, not the sidekick, not us. Readers try to solve the mystery along with everyone in the story. We share their ignorance and frustration and, when the solution is discovered, we applaud the solver. Let's call this kind of secret the "Sherlock Holmes."

The other kind of secret is known to the reader but not to everyone else. How many movie scenes have you watched with your hands over your eyes because you *know* the monster is lurking upstairs? How many times have you shouted, "Don't go in there!"? Snow White thinks the apple is safe to eat. Romeo thinks Juliet is dead. We know different. Let's call this kind of secret

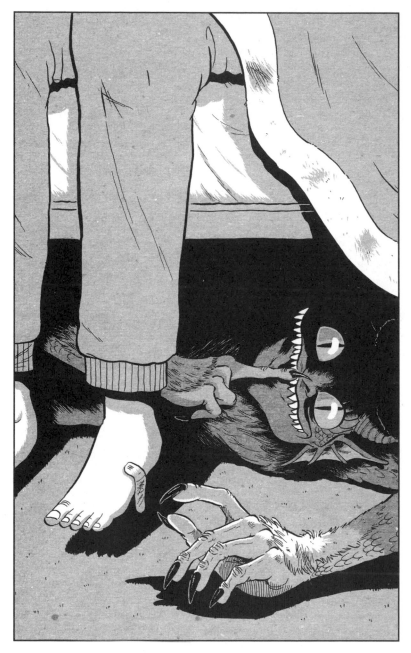

YOU *KNOW* THE MONSTER IS LURKING UPSTAIRS . . .

the "Clark Kent" because — well, you know why. The Clark Kent secret is a great way to bring readers into the story. Having more knowledge than some of the characters puts us closer to the center of the action. We are more invested.

It's super easy (see what I did there?) to set up a Clark Kent. Have the hero think or feel something. Readers are the only ones who will get the information. Of the four writing types, *insight* is pure Clark Kent.

Let's say that Michelle, the narrator, thinks a lot about Mike's smile and his funny stories. We know she likes Mike, but she's too shy to tell him, so he doesn't know. With this Clark Kent secret, we'll get more out of their next conversation.

"Hi, Mike," said Michelle. "Did you get a haircut?"

"Huh? No. Why, do I need one?"

"No, no. I was just —"

"Making a joke? Why?"

"Can I tell you something, Mike? My feelings are hard to put into words, but . . . well . . . what I'm trying to tell you is —"

"You're not perfect either, Michelle. There's a pimple on your forehead. And you wore that shirt yesterday. Talk about me getting a haircut — you could do with some grooming lessons too."

Your story may already have a secret. If it does, make sure you take full advantage of it to capture and keep our interest. Which brings me to the last item on my plot checklist. *Surprise* is a key ingredient in engagement. When you surprise us, we want to read on. If we already know what's going to happen, we'll get bored.

There are two kinds of surprises. One is the tiger trap. Someone is walking along and with no warning — BOOM! — falls into a hole. This kind of shock works well at the start of a story. Kiranmala wakes up on her birthday to find her parents gone and a rakkhosh demon in her kitchen. Aza Ray Boyle vanishes from her earthly sickbed and appears in Magonia, where she has all sorts of powers. The reader says, "Wow, I did NOT see that coming."

Check over your story for tiger traps. One is good. But you don't want too many pure surprises. Here's an example of too many tiger traps:

I was shooting hoops in my driveway when my basketball split open and I realized it was really a pterodactyl egg! The baby dinosaur took off, screeching, and was sucked into the engine of a fighter jet that appeared out of nowhere! The plane exploded, and suddenly the air was full of hundred-dollar bills . . .

Check the start and end of your story. Do you use a single tiger trap to set up a problem? That's probably enough.

The second type of surprise relates to character. It could go in the next chapter, but let's cover it now while we're talking about surprises. "Human Bites Dog" is news because it's a surprise — it's the opposite of what we expect to happen. Feel free to use that kind of surprise when you build characters. A grandma with a big smile, half-glasses and a plateful of cookies is not news. A grandma who farts and swears is more surprising. She can help build a story. In the same way, a bully doesn't have to be huge. A nerd doesn't have to wear glasses. Surprise the reader. Stretch your character ideas.

Speaking of which . . .

CHAPTER 19
CHARACTER CHECKLIST

Your rewrite is going to have to include a look at your characters. The most important of these is your hero, and that's who I talk about in this chapter. But the checklist applies to other major players: villains, sidekicks,

romantic interests. There are many ways to make a character credible and engaging. Here are three things you should be thinking about. Ask yourself: *Is my hero competent? Consistent? Hungry?*

Once again, we'll go into a bit of detail.

COMPETENCE

We like to read about people who do things well. Maybe your hero is a magician or superhero with amazing powers. It's easy to admire someone like that. But even if your main character is as normal as a glass of water, it'd be nice if they were good at something. A regular doofus (like me or many of my characters) could still be really funny, or really determined, or have an aptitude for math or football. Give them something!

Don't make your hero perfect. Achilles is invulnerable — except for his heel. Superman is the Man of Steel until he's exposed to kryptonite. Sherlock Holmes is an ideal thinking machine, but he's also a drug addict. Their weaknesses are part of the attraction. Make your hero competent, but give them a flaw as well.

CONSISTENCY

It's OK for characters to change their minds or attitudes during the course of the story. That's movement — that's great. But keep personalities consistent within a scene. If Chad is the sort of guy who only says "Yup . . . Nope . . . Huh . . ." don't give him unlikely lines when he's talking to Amanda about student council elections.

> *"Isn't democracy fascinating, Chad? I love flexing my voting muscles."*
>
> *"Uh-huh."*
>
> *"I mean, we're teenagers now, so we'll be voting for real in a few years. These elections give us a chance to practice. I've made up a list of questions for each of the candidates. Have you done likewise? Tell me, is there one issue you deem to be a priority?"*

Chad should not offer a cogent analysis of election issues here. Keep him consistent. His next line should be something like "Are you going to finish that donut?" Which is a nice segue into the most important thing about your main character. Rich or poor, superhero or schmuck, grumpy or happy (or Dopey or Doc), your main character must be hungry.

HUNGER

Heroes should *want* something. That's as important to the plot as something going wrong. Want pushes the story forward. If your hero wants to push her brother into the swimming pool, that leads to action. If your hero wants to escape from the giant spider, that leads to action too. As you reread the opening to your story, ask yourself what your main character wants. *That* is what your story is about. I want to meet Mom at the clothing store. I want to save Susie from the fire. If I don't want these things, there's no story. Dave and I will keep watching cartoons. The firefighters will rescue Susie and give her a lollipop. Ho hum.

Your story starts with what your hero wants, and it ends when they either get it or don't. Remember, there are a million ways to start a story, but only two ways to end it.

So far, the rewrite checklists have dealt with plot and character. How else can you improve your story? You can write better. Good style is almost impossible to define objectively. But I want to get across a few of my ideas about it. I'll take a deep breath and try to talk about the ineffable.

CHAPTER 20
WHAT IS GOOD STYLE?

A few years ago, my ten-year-old son and I watched one of the Transformers movie sequels (2? 3? I can't recall) together and had totally different responses. He loved it. I was so bored, I almost fell asleep.

Who was right?

We both were.

Your opinion of how good a painting or a movie or a book or a song is depends on your response. Were you interested, or bored? Did you laugh or cry, or did you yawn? Your response is valid but not objectively true. You can't prove it. Art is opinion, not fact. I can prove that the Great Pyramid of Cheops is around 450 feet high and made of 2,300,000 stone blocks. But I can't prove that it's cool.

It's the same with writing. There's no provable, sure-fire recipe for writing a stylish paragraph: *Take two declarative sentences and add a descriptive clause. Use three adjectives, a simile and a polysyllabic verb, and . . . voilà!* All you can do is write something *you* like, and hope others

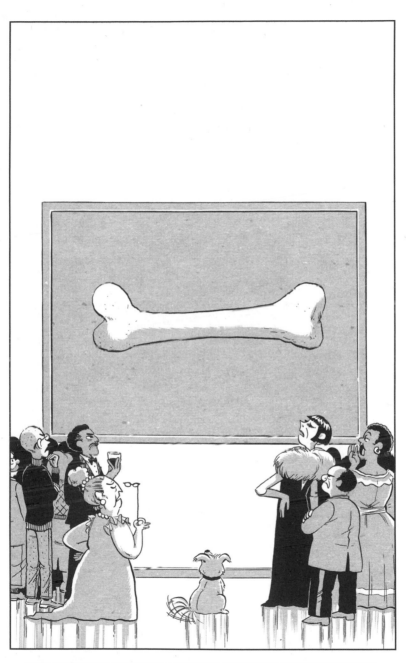

YOUR OPINION ON HOW GOOD A PAINTING IS DEPENDS ON YOUR RESPONSE.

like it too. Put yourself into it. The personal ingredient is what makes your writing true and real. Your best work sounds like you.

So there are no hard-and-fast rules for great writing. No guarantees. But there are a few basics you should be aware of. Like basic dress sense tells you not to wear stripes and checks and polka dots in the same outfit. That kind of thing. I'll talk a little about style basics, and you can try them as you work through your rewrite. Do you think they make your story better? Pay attention to what you think. Your opinion matters.

Yes it does.

CHAPTER 21
STYLE CHECKLIST

I'll talk about style from two different perspectives — the style of your story as a whole, and its component parts.

First, overall style. I talked about narrative versus scenes before, and I said I'd revisit the subject. Here we are. Most stories are a mix of telling and showing, of narration and scenes. You probably wrote your story this

way without thinking too much about it. Now I want you to think about it.

There is no right ratio, but beginner writers tend to be in a hurry to get to the end of their stories, so they use too much narrative and not enough scenes. My suggestion: Slow down. Enjoy the moment that a scene captures.

Here's an example of dashing through a story:

When I sprained my ankle, walking was a lot of work, so I used my little brother's wagon. I crashed, but it was Chyou's fault. My hospital bed had wheels too. . . .

As I'm writing this, it sounds like it could make a good story. But even I don't know what's going on. There should be details. Where was I going? What did I want to do when I got there? Who's Chyou? Adding dialogue, description and insight, making the crash a scene, then moving to the hospital, makes a better story.

Narration takes readers through your story faster. Scenes give them more enjoyment. If your story is a car trip with you driving, make sure you visit a rest stop every now and then. Let your readers go to the bathroom. Let them enjoy a sandwich or a scenic vista.

Style can hinge on the smallest things. I'm going to finish up the checklist by talking about the smallest component of your story — words. Are you using too many words?

MAKE SURE YOU VISIT A REST STOP EVERY NOW AND THEN.

Not enough? Are you using the right ones? Here are a couple of things to think about. Once again (again!), these are suggestions, not rules. But the suggestions come from someone who wants you to improve your writing, and who does this for a living. You're holding my book. Might as well consider my advice. And my advice is to pay attention to . . .

MODIFIERS

Modifiers add to our perception. They describe. A house becomes a *cozy little* house. Or a *haunted* house. Or a *burning* house. You can enter that house *hastily* or *reluctantly* or *noisily*.

Descriptors can be effective. Even very effective. But be careful. More is not better. One or two modifiers will do. Say that you are describing our old friend Steve. Now, Steve might be mean and lazy and tall and round-shouldered, with long black hair and tight jeans and a checked shirt and Chuck Taylors, but I don't know that I'd put all of those modifiers in the same sentence. For one thing, we're not going to remember them all. My advice is to find the most important thing about Steve and focus on that. Talk about how mean he is. Rat mean. Rusty-knife mean. No-candy-on-Halloween mean. Can you see him, with his graspy fingers and pinched mouth? What a meanie! Or if Steve's long hair is important for your story, focus on that. Talk about that black river flowing halfway down his back, rippling in the breeze like a flag, hiding his face like smoke.

Speaking of smoke, make sure your choice of modifier helps us to form a picture in our minds. For instance, what words would you normally use to describe smoke? Maybe *gray* or *black* or *drifting*, right? Since those words are already in our minds when we see the word *smoke*, don't use them to describe your smoke. We're already there. Give us a memorable picture. The Bible talks about a pillar of smoke. Charles Dickens talks about reluctant smoke. Reading these descriptions, we still see a gray cloud, but now it'll be standing straight and tall, or drifting up slowly.

Snow is white, grass is green, kittens are cute. Don't use modifiers that simply echo what we are already thinking. Add to that picture. Get more creative than that. The kitten is lop-eared or mean-spirited. Grass is thin or long or treacherous.

Be even more careful with adverbs. You know what adverbs are, right? They describe actions. Running *slowly*, talking *fast*, sighing *loudly*. Watch out for them. Here's a thought: When you come across a sentence with an adverb, try reading it without the adverb. If the sentence still works, you don't need the adverb. (Watch out for *suddenly*. That word gets a lot of use. Try your sentence without it. Works almost every time.)

My least favorite adverbs show up in dialogue.

> *"Hi, Mike! How's it going?" she asked brightly.*
> *"Fine, Michelle," he replied darkly. "Did you phone to tease me again? Because —"*
> *"Wait!" she interrupted urgently. "I want to apologize, Mike!"*
> *"Are you sure?" he said doubtfully.*
> *"Yes," she said decisively. "Yes I am."*

Yeesh. Lose all those adverbs. We don't need them. The dialogue itself tells us how the speaker is feeling.

VERBS

My third-grade teacher told us that a verb was a *doing* word. One kind of doing is talking. Remember how I told you that you don't need inquit phrases in writing dialogue, and to use *said* a lot because readers don't notice *said* and therefore pay attention to the dialogue? Remember that? Well, here's a twist. Because when it comes to other verbs — active ones — I want you to do the opposite. Use verbs we notice, verbs that make a picture.

Do not overuse common verbs. *Go,* for instance. *I was going to the store* does not give us a picture of the action. Were you walking, riding, driving? Were you on crutches, a skateboard, a pogo stick? Were you *dodging* raindrops or zombies? *Dragging* yourself to the store because your

mom asked you to get paper towels and you don't want to. Then *sprinting* because the store is about to close and Mom will kill you if you come home without paper towels. Each of those verbs give us a different picture of the journey. *Go* is one verb to watch for. Others: *do*, *get*, *make*, *take*. None of these verbs gives us a clear picture of what is going on. Listen — you can't avoid these verbs entirely. Don't overthink it. If you want to move your character to the store fast because an exciting thing happens after she gets there, then *I was going to the store* is fine. But if you want to give us a picture, if you want us to see her so we can identify with her, then another verb would be better.

ASSIGNMENT #8: REWRITE

Whew. That took a while, eh? Now it's time for you to do your rewrite.

Don't be overwhelmed. Read over your story. Check the plot — does it have a surprise? A secret? Check the main characters, especially the hero — are they consistent? Hungry? Do they have a flaw? And check your style — too fast or slow? Enough scenes to balance the narration? Too many modifiers? Most important, does it sound natural? Does it sound like you?

You're probably tired by now. That's natural. Sheesh, I'm tired and I do this for a living. But try not to resent the process. Reviewing and re-reviewing is part of writing, the same way drafting and re-drafting is part of art, and practicing the same sequence of notes over and over and over is part of playing music.

We're almost done here. Of course, you know that. Look where you are in the book — hardly any pages left.

THIS IS A HIGHLIGHT REEL OF THE BOOK.

CHAPTER 22
ALMOST DONE

Are you one of those people who flips ahead to the last chapter to find out how a story ends? My sister-in-law does that. "I want to know who I should pay attention to," she says.

If that's why you're here, you're in luck. This is a highlight reel of the book, summing up the whole thing in a few paragraphs. The ideas in this chapter are the takeaways, the things I want you to carry into your future with story — whether you're watching it, playing it, reading it, or writing it.

If you've read the book and done the assignments, this chapter will cement the lessons I want you to learn.

If not, this is what you missed. . . .

When you're writing a story, you:

• **PREPARE** by first finding an incident you care about. Something that happened to you or that you heard about, something that makes you angry or sad, scared or embarrassed. Remember that there's no story unless something goes wrong.

• **MODEL** using another story as a template for your own. In this book, I use one of my stories as a model. I compare a story to a pizza, using a crust (setting) you're familiar with, and toppings (characters) based on you and people you know. Set the oven dial to WHAT IF for a problem.

• **WRITE** your story in three parts. You set up the problem, make it worse, and finish with an ending that's both surprising and satisfying to readers. Then make sure you link the crisis and ending back to an earlier incident using a hook back.

• **REWRITE** your story, which means taking it apart and putting it back together. You make sure that your main character wants something, that the story is told in scenes as well as narration, with characters in conflict, and in a style that sounds like you.

Seems like a detailed process, eh? You've worked hard to get your story to the place it is now. Is it perfect? Nope.

But it's as good as you can make it for now. Which is all that any of us can say about our stories at any time.

Next time you read a book, think about how long it took the author to write it, how many times they had to go over it, to rethink ideas, to redo and re-redo. This book, for instance. A lot has changed from my first draft. And you have been part of the process. Yes, you. I approach the idea of story a little differently, thanks to you. Thinking about you all as I write, I have come to a new and better understanding of my own job.

So thank you. Thank you all.

Here's a related takeaway. This book is about story, which I've been thinking and talking about for years. But actually *writing* it — putting my thoughts down in black-and-white — has made me think differently. It sounds hokey, but every story is a journey of discovery, and the act of writing the story is part of that journey.

Less hokey, but just as critical, is this: The most important thing about telling a story isn't getting every word right. You won't. The most important thing is to make us care about your story, to make it engaging and convincing enough that we want to read on. And the best way to make *us* care about your story is for *you* to care. You have to believe it. It has to be your story, your truth.

Can you stretch that truth? Sure. You don't have to write about your actual day — brushing your teeth, yelling at your sister, getting a B– on your geography assignment, playing *Star Death Quest VII*, getting up in the middle of the night to go to the bathroom. You don't have to be your actual age, with your actual skill set, pet peeves and friends, living on your actual street. It's interesting and informative to stretch yourself, to try to inhabit someone who isn't quite you. One way to learn about yourself is to try to imagine how someone else would feel.

But —

And this is important —

The story must be convincing. Facts and events within the story don't have to be true, but the overall story must be authentic. Which means it must be true for you.

I often write from points of view that aren't mine. It's been a while since I was a teenager. I've never had an alien living in my nose (that I know of anyway). I've never sat beside a zombie. I've never had much trouble with spelling or grammar. And yet my teenaged narrators — who deal with alien visitors and zombie classmates, whose spelling is atrocious — every one of these narrators is very, very, *very* much like me. I react to life the same way they do. I laugh at the same things they do. I'm scared of the same things, sad about the same things, angry at the

same things. It's not just that I care about their stories —
they are my stories too.

Could a teenager write a convincing story of a parent
going through a divorce? I'm going to say no. Better for
the teen to write a story about a kid whose parents are
going through a divorce.

If you've lived your whole life in Yellowknife, could
you write a convincing story from the point of view of a
Haitian refugee? Be careful about telling someone else's
story instead of yours. The more of *you* there is in the story,
the more authentic it'll read. So if you're a born Yellowknifer
(is that the word?), or Vancouverite or Haligonian (yes, that
is the word), and you make friends with a Haitian refugee,
write that story instead: *When Roseline first came to the class,
I didn't like her. She was always frowning. Later, I realized that
she was just shy. . . .* If you want to stretch yourself, maybe
write a story about your family adopting a refugee. How
would you feel about Roseline if she were your new sister?
Suddenly having to share a bathroom and closet. Having
to take Roseline skating, and listening to Mom go *ooh* and
ahh over her French accent. . . . Lots of this can be made
up, but it's about you. It would still be your story.

Reading other people's stories is a way we learn about
each other and ourselves. I am currently reading a memoir

written by a teen from a war-torn country. I am aghast, horrified and full of admiration for him. His life is nothing like mine. And yet there are moments of connection, of shared experience. At one point in the story, he is running from a troop of soldiers who want to kill him when he comes across a garden full of hibiscus flowers. The quickest route would take him through the garden, but he goes around it instead. You see, when he was younger he got in trouble for trampling his mom's garden, and he doesn't want that to happen again. Which is exactly what happened to me when I was a kid, and exactly how I felt.

We're all human. Much more unites us than divides us. Let's understand our shared truth even as we appreciate our differences. The better we get to know each other, the better we'll get along. An informed society is an inclusive society. And an inclusive society is the only one worth living in.

Discovering other people's stories is only half of sharing. Other people should read your story too. Which is why your story matters. Yes it does.

AFTERWORD: FAQ

If I was doing an author visit at your school (or church or writing circle or service club or whatever organization you belong to — seriously, I'll talk to anyone), then here is where you'd get to ask questions.

Let's scoot quickly over the most common ones. There's always someone who asks how much money I make (answer: not enough), and how old I am (answer: very). Several people will want to know where I get my ideas from (if you've read this book you know the answer to that) and if I'm friends with Stephen King or Oprah or someone like that (answer: no). Some kid might ask if I know the answer to a riddle, like *What has four fingers and*

a thumb but is not alive? (Me: *I don't know, what?* The kid: *A glove! Hahahaha.*) There might be a question about my favorite food or color or book or movie (answers vary, but right now: black licorice, ecru, *How Tom Beat Captain Najork and His Hired Sportsmen*, *The Lady Eve*).

Every now and then, I hear a really good question. A couple years ago, a kid at the back of a high school auditorium got my attention by asking if I was having fun right then, during question time at her school. I told her the truth, which is that I try to get as much as I can out of every moment, and that right then I was having a whole lot of fun. "Connecting with people through story is one of my favorite things," I said.

She had a follow-up.

"What's the most fun you've ever had, talking about writing?"

And since this book talks about writing, and since I started out by saying that stories are fun, I think it's an appropriate way to tie the book together if I give you the same answer I gave that high school student. Remember Ralph and the "Hero Meets Dog" assignment? Here's the story. . . .

One of my funnest moments ever came during a talk with a group of first graders. I was tired after a full day of presentations, and the teacher-librarian had poured me a cup of coffee. (No, you do not have to pay attention to the cup of coffee. I'm just setting the scene here.)

The kids and I were building a story together, starting with characters and setting. We had a boy and a dog running across a field, and we were working out how they could relate to each other. "Is the boy afraid of the dog?" I asked. "Does the dog save the boy's life? Does the boy smuggle the dog into his room because his parents won't let him have one?"

I wanted to get across the importance of surprise. It's a more interesting story when we don't know what's going to happen next. So I asked the first graders to think of a surprising way for the dog and boy to get together. *What could happen that we don't expect to happen?*

A redheaded boy sitting at the back of the story-time circle got up on his knees and started waving his hand around.

"I know," he said, eyes wide behind his glasses. "I know, I know!"

"What's your idea, Ralph?" I asked. He had waved his hand around enough times by then that I knew his name.

Ralph spread his arms wide and stared ahead like he was on the deck of the *Titanic*, or pretending to be a bird.

"*I think*," he said, "that the boy should *catch* the dog. And then . . ."

He paused.

"Yes," I said.

"*Then* I think the boy should take the dog *home*. And then . . ."

He paused again. He had a honking nasal voice, like he had swallowed a tiny microphone, or was just getting over croup. I took a sip of coffee. The class was quiet.

". . . And *then* I think the boy should *eat* the dog."

Ralph sat back with a smile. The class shrieked — maybe because I had done a spit take and got coffee on myself. I wiped my pants and mouth. And cleared my throat.

"That would be a surprise, all right," I said.

"*Especially*," he said, "for the dog."

A writer's job is to engage readers. One of the best ways to do this is to present an unexpected event from an unexpected point of view. Ralph was absolutely right. The boy knows he's going to eat the dog. It's no surprise to him. It *is* a surprise to the dog, and to us.

By sharing his story idea, Ralph made me a better writer.

I often get asked what advice I can give aspiring writers. I tell them to read, and imitate, and try and fail and try again. I tell them to care about what they write, to start

"... AND *THEN* I THINK THE BOY SHOULD *EAT* THE DOG."

their stories with truth, create a problem and not solve it, and end in a way that brings readers back to the beginning of the story. I tell them to engage with their readers by making the story interesting and clear. All the things I talk about in this book.

And I often quote Ralph. Somewhere in your story, I say, try to include a boy-eats-dog moment. At the time, I applauded Ralph, and laughed along with the rest of the first graders. I laughed some more on the way home from Ralph's school. I'm smiling right now as I write this.

I get satisfaction from accomplishment. I enjoy eating and drinking and running around. I like connecting with others. I look forward to trying new things. I enjoy playing games. But nothing is as much fun as story.

APPENDIX 1

BEST STORY-BUILDING EXERCISES EVER

Here are two exercises that combine character construction and plot building. I have used them in workshops and as aids in my own writing. The first exercise is borrowed and adapted from one of Isabel Huggan's. The second is a modification of Georges Simenon's professed writing technique. He wrote over two hundred books this way.

DEDUCTIVE

Deductive means "from the top down." We are starting with an ideal or universal and working from that. In this case, a portrait. Take a look at it. This is a picture of our hero. See them? I want to know three things about them. (Don't worry, there are no wrong answers here.) First: What is their name? Write it down. Second thing: What do they do? They look young enough to be a student, and that's a good answer. But they could also be a model, actor, caregiver, spy, checkout clerk, YouTuber, superhero. And now for the third thing. Think about this: What is their secret? Give them something to worry about.

In short: Who are they, what do they do, and what are they hiding from the world?

That's our main character. But no one exists on their own. Relationships are vital to story. So now (holding up portrait #2) give this character a name, too, and explain their relationship to our main character. Are they a relative? Neighbor? Customer? Crush?

These two folks are a good start, but we don't have a story yet. For that we need to have some kind of conflict. And, as you remember, conflict is shaped like a triangle. What I want you to do now is invent a character to act as the third corner of a conflict involving the two you've already invented. I want you

to come up with someone who will mess up the relation-ship. Baby, rival, mugger, love interest, puppy, mysteri-ous stranger who turns out to be a relative? This will probably involve the revelation or potential revelation of the hero's secret.

And that's the start of a story. You're welcome.

INDUCTIVE

If *deductive* means from the general to the particular — that is, from the top down — *inductive* is the opposite. Here we're building from the bottom up, adding pieces together to make a whole. We'll describe their most inti-mate and personal space — their bedroom.

This is where your main character sleeps. Let's start at the bottom. What kind of floor? Hardwood? Linoleum? Broadloom? Is it a ship's deck? Or a spaceship's? Is it snow or dirt in a quinzhee or cave? Cold prison concrete? Smelly dumpster steel?

Now we move to the bed itself. Is it a twin or double, queen or king? Is it a crib or hospital cot? Is it a bed of nails? A hammock? Is it ten feet of piled mattresses with a pea under the bottom one?

On to the shoes under the bed. They belong to your main character. What do they wear? Sneakers, sandals,

Crocs, stilettos, knee-high pirate boots? Size 2? Size 8B? Size 18EEE?

There's a window in the room. What does it look out on? A suburban backyard? A rat-infested alley? A heaving ocean? Deep space? A prison exercise yard? Versailles in seventeenth-century France?

On a table next to the bed are three small personal items, things your character wears or carries around all the time. What are they? Diary, comb, keys, phone, jewelry,

slingshot, favorite pen, sunglasses, astrolabe, snuff horn? You decide.

Finally, I want you to focus on the three most important connections in your character's life. If there's a phone, who were the last three callers? If this room predates phones, who wrote the last three letters? If the room is post-phones, who is at the other end of the last three communications by hologram or teleporter or AI#sp&ch or whatever? Not just names — give us a sense of the connection. Who are the most important people in your character's daily life? Mom, boyfriend, parole officer, Starfleet Command, Grampa, bookie, pizza delivery person, Dungeon Master?

And now — having established what their bedroom looks like in some detail — *now* you can go about giving your character a name and occupation. Who are they, what do they do?

These exercises can give some depth to characters you may not know very well. But a fully realized character is not a plot. Here's how you make one: Write a message to the character you just created that will totally change their life.

Any kind of message can work here: an email or text, posted letter or social media comment, an artifact from the past, a hint from the future, a telegram, a smoke signal or an overheard comment. The idea is to make this new information the inciting incident for your story — the thing that sets it in motion.

For example, the message could be from the cancer clinic asking your hero to call back as soon as possible. It could come from a lawyer or long-lost relative telling your hero that they are suddenly rich — or poor. It could come from a casting agent saying the part is theirs. An overheard conversation could reveal that a mutual friend or coworker has a huge crush on your hero. A disembodied voice could say, simply, "Save France," or "Kill them all," or "Go to the window now."

Stories deal with change. Change starts with an inciting incident. Here's yours. You're ready to start writing.

APPENDIX 2

NOTES ON STORIES I MENTION

PART 1: PREPARING

P. 4 – *SpongeBob SquarePants* is a cartoon set at the bottom of the sea. Note how often things get worse in each eleven-minute episode. These are seriously busy plots!

P. 10 – Jean Valjean is the hero of *Les Misérables*, one of my least favorite classics. There are famous scenes and memorable characters, but the story drags and wanders. Hilariously, it's at least two hundred pages before we meet our hero.

P. 19 – *The Two Towers* is book 2 of *The Lord of the Rings*, maybe the most influential and stylishly written epic ever. Many fantasy novels borrow from Tolkien, who was himself reusing Scandinavian lore. A whole lot of guy characters, hardly any gals. At sixteen, *LOTR* was my favorite book.

P. 19 – *The Hobbit*, also by Tolkien, also influential and well written. Dwarves, elves, trolls, wizards, dragons, plenty of hobbits. I cannot recall a female character with a speaking part except, maybe, the spiders in Mirkwood Forest.

P. 21 – *The Nose from Jupiter* is my first book for kids. The smart-alecky alien, Norbert, is a thinly disguised version of me.

P. 24 – *Downside Up* is another book of mine. Darker than my usual style, one of my faves.

P. 27 – "The Three Little Pigs" is a classic fairy tale with rising action. The stakes get higher and higher . . . and higher. Disney's 1933 *Silly Symphony* was the first movie my dad ever saw, and it scared him rigid. Ahhh, simpler times.

P. 27 – "Little Red Riding Hood" is maybe my favorite fairy tale, with a great sneak-type villain! Check out Michael Emberley's version, *Ruby*.

P. 28 – Holden Caulfield is a whiny teen on a hero's journey in *The Catcher in the Rye*. We like him because he's funny, tells the truth and hates hypocrisy. The only super-popular book I can think of that has never been adapted into a movie.

P. 28 – Parvana, the hero of *The Breadwinner* and its se-quels, is an eleven-year-old Afghani who takes on an op-pressive regime. Note how she is *different* because she is a girl, and also how she is different from other girls. The message is uplifting and relevant.

P. 28 – Claireece "Precious" Jones is a teen with a yucky personal life. "My Happiest Day" makes a lousy story. Claireece's genuinely unhappy "day" makes *Push* hard to read, but it's a rewarding story.

P. 29 – *Me & Death* is my least popular book. Dunno why. Wait, I do. But I can't say here.

P. 29 – *Zomboy*'s central idea came to me in a flash: *What if* the new kid, sitting beside you, was a zombie? Everything flows from that.

P. 33 – Bugs Bunny is one of the best-known cartoon heroes. He's a smart aleck who always wins, even when he's up against a shotgun or charging bull. One way to make your character memorable is to give them a signature tagline. "Bah! Humbug!" or "My precious" or "What's up, Doc?"

P. 35 – The Grinch and Horton are more complete characters, but *The Cat in the Hat* is one of the purest "stranger comes to town" plots in all fiction.

P. 35 – Sky Woman is the key figure in the Haudenosaunee creation story. She's not striving for female empowerment or creativity — she has it to start with.

P. 35 – The Beast is, of course, from *Beauty and the Beast*. There are lots of story versions out there, but most of us know the movie — one of Disney's best. Note the attention to the minor characters (who are more interesting than the heroes). And remember: Your hero should want something. The stakes matter here.

P. 35 – Snow White's story is, again, best known through the Disney film. Again, the hero is boring and the villain and minor characters are pretty good.

P. 35 – *The Little Mermaid* is one of Hans Christian Andersen's best stories, where Ariel gives up everything to win her prince and a human soul, and things get quite dire. Disney makes it all sentimental. But the villain and minor characters are fun, and the songs help.

P. 35 – Lucy is the hero and our moral voice in *The Lion, the Witch and the Wardrobe.* This is a great "portal" story — movement through a magical wardrobe into another world. There's betrayal and talking animals. This was the first chapter book I read on my own.

P. 35 – *Romeo and Juliet* is so famous you know something about it even if you haven't read the play or seen the movies. Lovers not allowed to meet due to stupid family prejudice. It's important for your story to have a problem, and this is a biggie. Spoiler alert: it ends badly.

P. 35 – Rapunzel is famous because of one thing. Try to make the hero of your story noteworthy. Pick one feature and play it up. Can you think of anything memorable about Rapunzel? Yeah, you can.

P. 35 – *Cinderella* is a classic evil stepmom story. The original gets pretty grim (haha, get it? Grim? Grimm?) with the stepsisters cutting off bits of their own feet to fit into the slipper. Try to make your hero *do* more than Cinderella. The prince does all the work. She reminds me of Bella from *Twilight.*

P. 35 – Odysseus is the hero of *The Odyssey*, maybe the most famous journey plot. In fact, *odyssey* has come to mean "a long journey." Like Dorothy, Odysseus wants to get home. The story starts in the middle, on Calypso's island, then goes back to explain how they got there. Not a bad technique.

P. 35 – Jonah gets swallowed by a whale in one of the best-known stories in the Bible, which is full of great stories. Stakes are high: flood, famine, war, plague, banishment, betrayal, crucifixion. Lots of secrets and surprises. More girls than there are in Tolkien, but not a lot of girl power. (Just saying.)

P. 35 – Lara Croft is the hero of the *Tomb Raider* franchise. I am not much of a gamer. The video games I talk about are the ones my kids beat me at, or else they're so famous that even I have heard of them. Lara is an Indiana Jones–type action hero, who *does* way more than Cinderella or Rapunzel.

P. 35 – The Rythulian Traveler is the hero of the *Journey* video game. The plot is indeed a journey, but in this game, setting matters. Characters can work together but you don't know each other.

P. 38 – *The Karate Kid* was a movie first, then a TV show. A kid becomes an amazing warrior with the help of an unconventional instructor. Sounds like *The Empire Strikes Back*, or the entire Harry Potter franchise, doesn't it?

PART 2: MODELING

P. 43 – Pippi Longstocking is the muscular hero of nine (I think) stories. I like how non-epic the plots are, and how calm Pippi is. Like Sky Woman, she takes her power for granted. Like Anne Shirley, she rocks the red braids.

P. 43 – Pecola Breedlove is the hero of *The Bluest Eye*, a family story where bad things happen to people who go on and do horrible things themselves. It's not fair and it doesn't end well for anyone, but especially not for Pecola. The writing is about as good as writing gets.

P. 43 – Frenchie is the hero of *The Marrow Thieves*, which is a coming-of-age story featuring real-world nastiness toward Indigenous peoples, and fantasy elements that are both cool and distressing. A book to make you mad.

P. 58 – Discworld is a series of stories that take place on a flat planet made up by Terry Pratchett. Fantasy is not always funny. J.R.R. Tolkien, Robert Jordan and N.K. Jemisin are great fantasy writers, but not funny. Terry Pratchett is really funny.

P. 58 – Rokugan is the setting for the *Legend of the Five Rings* game. Lots of clear geographical and social details. *L5R* can be a card game or a Dungeons-and-Dragons-style RPG. Plot varies.

P. 58 – Wakanda is an Afro-futuristic land rich in a mysterious and powerful element which plays a key role in the movie *Black Panther*. I'm the wrong guy to ask about it since I am not much of an MCU fan.

P. 59 – *The Simpsons* is a long-running TV series that has become part of Western culture. You know it, I know it. Occasionally I'll run across someone who says they don't like the show, or never found it funny. I nod and walk quietly away.

P. 61 – Westeros is the setting for *Game of Thrones*. The books and TV series feature great characters, and famously unexpected plot twists that can be summed up in the idea that no one is safe.

P. 66 – *Winnie-the-Pooh* introduced the famous characters, who show up again in *The House at Pooh Corner*. Character, style and philosophy are more important than plot in these stories. I suggest reading the originals rather than the Disney makeovers.

P. 66 – Jemima Puddle-Duck is the hero of one of my two favorite Beatrix Potter stories. (*The Tale of Peter Rabbit* is the other one.) The sneaky villain is the same as the one in "Little Red Riding Hood."

P. 66 – Snoopy is a popular member of the Peanuts gang. I like the way he is both a dog who sleeps outside and also a "human" who collects art, wins arguments and lives a rich fantasy life.

P. 66 – Mr. Toad is a funny blowhard character in *The Wind in the Willows*. He is important to the plot because he wants things and acts (not always wisely) to make them happen. He is a lot like *South Park*'s Cartman, and fills the same role.

PART 3: WRITING

P. 101 – Hamlet is the hero and the name of the play. Like Rapunzel, he's got a definite look. He wears black, holds a skull and pretends to be crazy.

P. 104 – *Imogene's Antlers* is a picture book with the whole plot in the opening line. It's easy story building. Change one important thing about yourself, then imagine various ways the change could complicate your life. There's your plot.

P. 105 – Daffy Duck is one of my favorite cartoon heroes. He thinks he's amazing and he loses every time. Daffy and Bugs Bunny and the gang have been around forever. Fun childhood memories involve watching them with my dad, who laughed as hard as me and my brother did.

P. 105 – Dick Dastardly is a baddie in a cartoon called *Wacky Races*. Stereotypes can work when you're writing comedy. I laughed every time Dick twirled his moustache.

P. 105 – Bullwinkle J. Moose is one of the heroes in *The Adventures of Rocky and Bullwinkle and Friends*, a cartoon with some very "smart," funny writing. Classic comic pairing: Small clever character and big dumb one. Asterix and Obelix, Bart and Homer Simpson.

P. 114 – *Fantasia* is a feature-length cartoon telling stories using only classical music — a bold idea at the time it was made. "The Sorcerer's Apprentice" has the strongest plot, but it's all fun to look at.

P. 114 – *The Wizard of Oz* is the only movie I've ever been really scared of. The book's good too. Great setting, pretty cool characters and one of the best plots of all time.

P. 114 – *Super Mario Odyssey* is a game that takes you through a series of worlds featuring the gang in different fantastic settings and narratives. The aspect of the story that I like best involves not knowing what is real.

P. 114 – *Portal* is a video game where *making it worse* is most of the plot. You're trying to escape, and each puzzle is harder to solve.

P. 129 – Wile E. Coyote is one of the best-known losers ever, despite never saying a word. With all his elaborate contraptions, he never catches the Road Runner. Usually stories focus around the hero. Not here. Wile E. is way more interesting.

P. 131 – *Alice in Wonderland* does not have a driving plotline, which may be why it has never really worked as a movie. But who cares about plot? It has great scenes with brilliant dialogue from iconic characters.

P. 131 – *Where the Wild Things Are* is a picture book that takes our hero on a journey of imagination where he confronts his own monsters. Great art and a dreamy plotline.

P. 132 – My camping trips were mostly fun. In *Noses Are Red*, I imagined what would happen if things went really wrong. Our loser hero needs lots of help and gets it from unexpected sources.

PART 4: REWRITING

P. 143 – Sherlock Holmes is the most famous detective ever. He calls it "deduction," but he's actually working inductively, building upward from small details to a whole solution. Great example of the narrator not being the star. This is how you tell the story of a character who is not like you: *tell your story as their friend*.

P. 145 – Clark Kent looks normal but has amazing powers. He is vulnerable to an element from his past. Superman is the classic superhero.

P. 146 – *Kiranmala* is a TV series based on folktales from Bengal. A tough-talking princess hero saves the world from an evil queen.

P. 146 – *Magonia* is a novel set in a land above the clouds, where our gasping, dying hero is healthy and powerful. Will she be able to save the earth in the upcoming war?

P. 152 – *Transformers: Revenge of the Fallen* is — I think — the film my son and I saw. Hero saves the world and goes to college. I had trouble telling the bots apart. "Are the Decepticons the spiky ones?" I asked Ed, who did not even bother to reply.

P. 172 – *How Tom Beat Captain Najork and His Hired Sportsmen* is a long picture book about, well, fooling around. Best descriptions ever of made-up games: totally convincing without giving any idea of what is going on.

P. 172 – *The Lady Eve* is a 1940's movie written and directed by Preston Sturges, one of my faves. It is slapstick funny, clever and thoughtful. Sturges is admired and imitated by the Coen brothers — two more of my faves.